THE COMPLETE
SLOW COOKER
COOKBOOK

Cara Hobday

10 9 8 7 6 5 4 3 2 1

This omnibus edition published in 2014 by Ebury Press, an imprint of Ebury Publishing
The Ultimate Slow Cooker Cookbook published in 2009 and Ultimate Slow Cooker Favourites
published in 2010 by Ebury Press, an imprint of Ebury Publishing

A Random House Group Company

The Random House Group Limited Reg. No. 954009

Addresses for companies within the Random House Group can be found at
www.randomhouse.co.uk

A CIP catalogue record for this book is available from the British Library.

The Random House Group Limited supports the Forest Stewardship Council® (FSC®), the leading
international forest-certification organisation. Our books carrying the FSC label are printed on FSC®-
certified paper. FSC is the only forest-certification scheme supported by the leading environmental
organisations, including Greenpeace. Our paper procurement policy can be found at
www.randomhouse.co.uk/environment

To buy books by your favourite authors and register for offers visit www.randomhouse.co.uk

Printed and bound in China by C&C Offset Printing Co., Ltd

ISBN 9780091957995

Design: Isobel Gillan
Photography: Rob White
Food styling: Cara Hobday (www.carahobday.com) and Phil Mundy
Prop stylists: Tessa Evelegh and Luis Peral
Copy editor: Emma Callery

Contents

Introduction 4

Soups and light meals 12

Easy midweek suppers 57

Vegetarian and vegetable dishes 107

Cooking for friends 148

Weekend pot roasts 205

Puddings and desserts 219

Preserves 233

Index 238

Introduction

The soothing smell of a pot that has been simmering slowly for hours, filling the house with rich aromas and the promise of a welcoming supper, is the ultimate end to a long day and one of the comforts of home.

For this reason alone, many people are rediscovering their slow cookers. Dusted off and plugged in, they are perfect for the hectic schedules of modern life. Whether you are working late, off to football practice, just in from college, or simply wanting to eat dinner as a family with minimum fuss, putting aside just 15 minutes in the morning to assemble your evening meal means that you can have a hot supper on the table moments after you walk through your door.

Of course, there are other reasons why people might choose to invest in a slow cooker. Nowadays, we are aware that eating healthily is important to our wellbeing. We also know that convenience foods are not the answer; we would all prefer to serve up home-cooked food rather than a shop-bought ready-meal. With a slow cooker in your kitchen armoury, you can enjoy a wholesome hot meal at the end of every day, rather than resort to supermarket convenience foods or compromise on health.

Slow cookers can also provide a very economical way of cooking. Generous meals can be made from thrifty cuts of meat. Simmered for hours, these otherwise forsaken cuts give up all their flavour to the dish, staying succulent while still providing you and your family with all the nutrition you need. Just add some potatoes or bread and you have a truly frugal feast.

Choosing the less popular (read 'cheaper') cuts of meat, such as oxtail, beef shins or delicious lamb middle neck chops, also means that you can choose higher-quality, (read 'organic') meat more often. You can therefore eat well, with a clear social conscience, and without breaking the bank balance.

Although the slow cooker is re-establishing itself in our homes, the recipe books that our mothers used all those years ago do not necessarily provide us with the tastes we want today. We eat differently now: we expect texture and colour in our food, fresh herbs, spices and cosmopolitan influences. We are familiar with the cooking of India, China and Mexico, and the flavours of Spain, Italy and France, and we want to be able to cook like this too. With this in mind, I have gathered up ideas and recipes from around the world, from the school playground and from many other slow-cooker users who have shared their tips with me, so that you can enjoy contemporary recipes in your slow cooker. So, whether you're feeding two or 20, throwing a Friday night curry together for friends, or simply putting the family dinner on before going out for the day, I hope that these recipes inspire you and show you how easy it is to eat well, with minimum fuss and time in the kitchen, every night of the week.

Buying a slow cooker

When browsing in kitchenware departments, you might previously have passed by the slow cookers, thinking they were not for you. But think again and consider how one might fit into your lifestyle.

Slow cookers are available to suit all households – big and small – and all budgets. Despite obvious differences in size, design and style, all slow cookers have two principal components: a ceramic pot and an element in the base that heats up the pot to a temperature that can cook the contents over several hours.

Slow cookers are available in a wide range of sizes, from the tiny 1 litre model – almost a flask – to the large 6.5 litre countertop version with a brushed stainless steel finish, which looks smart enough to leave out on the work surface. Some are heavy and not moved easily, while others are niftily light and easily portable, which can be useful for taking on a self-catering holiday, for example. Some models have ceramic cooking pots that are designed to be brought to the table, while the contents of others will have to be transferred to another container if you wish to serve the dish at the table.

All these design points are valued by different people in different ways, but one feature that I would recommend to include on your list is a timer. If the slow cooker has a timer, it switches itself to a safe holding temperature when cooking is finished. Apart from the obvious saving in electricity, this avoids overcooking the dish. Although it is difficult to overcook foods in the slow cooker, it can be done if left to cook for long past the correct time. Cook dishes for up to eight hours, then leave to stand for a maximum of two hours. The food could be held in the slow cooker for longer, but the flavours become subdued and indistinguishable, and the textures soften. One cooker that I think has a particularly good timer is the Cuisinart Cook 'n' Hold.

If you are a household of two, I would also advise you to think carefully before automatically choosing the smallest size of cooker, as you might come to find its capacity limiting. Consider how nice it can be to have leftovers for lunch the next day, a meal for later in the week, or simply a batch of casserole to put in the freezer. If you are a student or on a limited income, however, a small slow cooker, with its low running costs, could be ideal.

The 3.5 litre model is, I think, the most versatile. If you are a household of four, or are a growing family of two adults and several little ones, this is the size you are most likely to need. It offers room to make an ample 6–8 servings for a family dinner, with scope to freeze any leftovers. This model will fit a whole chicken quite neatly, or 6–8 adult portions of a side dish. The recipes in this book are written for the 3.5 litre size but can be adapted for the smaller or larger sizes by halving or doubling the quantities.

For a bigger household, or for when there are often more than three or four people for dinner, a 6 litre slow cooker is worth the investment of (not much) extra money and the additional space that it will take up in your kitchen. While 6 litres is a large capacity, don't forget that the actual dishes usually fill the cookers to only halfway, and the extra space is needed for stirring and bubbling. This size will happily accommodate all possible uses for the slow cooker – parties, evening meals, soups and preserves. Don't imagine that you have to fill up the 6 litre slow cooker every time you use it. Although the recipes in this book can be doubled when cooking for 10 or 12, a dish for 6–8 portions can also be cooked in this size without a problem.

Energy usage

With price fluctuations, environmental concerns and shortages, our energy usage and the need to reduce our consumption is an everyday issue. Using a slow cooker instead of an oven is one very easy way to save energy. The average slow cooker uses around 240 watts of energy, compared with the average oven, which uses 700 watts, and cooking over the hob, which uses even more. This is quite a saving when added up over the course of a year.

The most energy-efficient models are those with the most insulation. Look for designs that are not hot to touch. Apart from the safety factor, this means that more of the heat is being kept in rather than wasted.

Caring for your slow cooker

- Before putting your slow cooker in the dishwasher, check the manufacturers' instructions. While most of the ceramic cooking dishes, and the lids, can go into the dishwasher, there are always exceptions. Ensure, too, that the dish is dry before placing it back in the unit.

- Do not transfer the ceramic dish straight from the refrigerator to the oven, as the sudden heat change will make it crack. Instead, keep your prepared ingredients in a separate dish, and spoon into the ceramic cooking dish when ready to cook. If transferring the hot ceramic dish to the refrigerator, wait until it cools to room temperature first.

- Most of the ceramic dishes cannot be used under the grill or in the oven because the high temperature causes them to crack.

Using your slow cooker

As well as using the recipes in this book, a wide variety of others can be adapted for use in a slow cooker, so you will still be able to cook those family favourites, and be inspired by other ideas. Look for recipes that have a sauce with them and can take long, slow cooking, ideally using a tougher cut of meat so it will benefit from the long cooking. Chicken that is cooked on the bone will work well, as in Spanish Chicken with Olives (see page 158), as will other cuts of meat on the bone, such as the lamb middle neck chops in Lancashire Hotpot (see page 73).

Tender cuts of meat do dry out during the long, slow cooking process, so it is a good idea to replace them in your recipe with tougher, cheaper cuts, and let the slow cooking tenderise them and create succulence. Replace lamb chops with the tougher and cheaper lamb middle neck chops, use pork shoulder in place of pork loin fillet or pork chops, and buy stewing or braising steak rather than rump steak. Replace tender chicken breast with chicken thighs. For meat to remain succulent and not dry out, it should be cut into cubes of approximately 2 cm. Don't worry if you have bought pre-cut meat of a different size; it will still give a good result.

When adapting a recipe for your slow cooker, I would recommend reducing the amount of liquid by a third initially and then add more liquid later, if needed.

This is because a slow cooker is completely sealed and does not lose any liquid during cooking, unlike oven or hob cooking. As a general rule of thumb, use around 600 ml of liquid in a dish for six servings, although this does vary between recipes, depending on other ingredients. If there are a lot of vegetables, for example, less liquid is needed, as the vegetables release their own water into the sauce. The Piripiri Chicken (see page 161), for instance, has hardly any liquid at the start of cooking, but by the time it has finished, it has a good amount of sauce from the peppers and onions.

Although pies with their crusty pastry cannot be made in the slow cooker, pie fillings are very successful. All you need to do is fill a pie dish with the slow-cooked filling, top it with pastry and finish it off in the oven.

You can even use your slow cooker for dishes that you might least think of trying. For example, you could cook your porridge in the slow cooker overnight for a ready-made hot breakfast in the morning. In the slow cooker container, just stir together your usual mix of porridge ingredients – mine is equal quantities of milk, water and oats – adding salt if desired. Then just leave on the low setting to cook overnight. In the morning, give it a stir before eating the delicious hot porridge.

Cooking for a crowd

When you are cooking for a crowd, a slow cooker is a real asset. You can use it for the tasks that are often the hardest to co-ordinate when cooking in large quantities: make the soup or the main dish during the day and keep it warm until ready to serve, or turn to it for cooking the rice or carbohydrate part of the meal, maybe the Lebanese Pilaf with Wholegrains (see page 116), or taking care of the dessert, perhaps Baked Cherry Cheesecake or Chocolate Custard Pots (see pages 228 and 230).

Leftovers

When a dish has been cooked in the slow cooker for the recommended time, you can treat any leftovers in the same way as dishes cooked by other means. Spoon them into lidded, freezable containers straight away so that they cool down as quickly as possible. Clearly mark the lid with the name of the dish, date and any reheating instructions. When cooled down to room temperature, the containers can then be frozen for up to one month. This is with the exception of rice, which can be the cause of food poisoning, so discard any leftovers.

Reheat the frozen meal in the microwave, on the hob or in the oven. The saucepan method might need a little water to be added. If using foil trays, these can be put straight into the oven after loosening the lid a little. Keep checking the dish as it is reheating, as some of the recipes might require a little water to be added.

Top tips for best results

Cooking

- Spray the ceramic pot with an oil spray or coat the bottom with oil before you put anything inside it, as this prevents the contents from sticking.

- If your recipe calls for a high amount of dairy products, such as milk, cream or yoghurt, there is a possibility they will curdle if left to cook for a long time. To avoid this, stir in the dairy products during the final 15 minutes of cooking, or substitute with evaporated or dried skimmed milk.

- One complaint against slow cookers is that meals can taste very similar. For this reason, it is important to brown the meat and the vegetables first, to draw the maximum flavour out of each ingredient. This also seals the meat, which prevents it drying out. When time is short, you can bypass the browning stage, but the taste of the finished dish might not be as flavoursome. Always brown minced meat over a high heat to kill any bacteria before adding to the pot.

- Be careful not to use too much water, as the sauce may not be thick enough in the final dish. Remember that no water is lost from the pot during cooking, and a lot of moisture comes out of the vegetables, which means that it won't boil dry.

- For added liquid, I use hot stock so that the slow cooker heats up more quickly. However, over a cook time of 8 hours, this is not essential and will not noticeably change the finished dish.

Holding

- The holding feature is one of the most useful on a slow cooker. If you intend to use it, note that where a recipe tells you to stir in an ingredient shortly before the end of cooking time (for instance, the tomatoes in Goan Fish Curry on page 61 are added '10 minutes before the end of cooking time'), it is usually fine to take that to mean '10 minutes before serving time'. Where there are exceptions (just two of the recipes), I've added the appropriate instructions.

Safety

- Never leave the slow cooker near the edge of the worktop where little fingers can touch the hot surface.

- Do not use your slow cooker for reheating leftovers as the temperature isn't hot enough.

Time-saving

- If time is short in the morning, prepare the dish the night before. Chill the components separately, but do not chill the ceramic pot from the cooker, as it might crack when reheated.

- Take your slow cooker on self-catering holidays: you can enjoy an extra hour on the beach or a spontaneous walk on the cliff, knowing that your next meal is happily bubbling away

Notes on the recipes

- All herbs are fresh, unless described otherwise.

- All vegetables are medium-sized, unless described otherwise.

- All fruit and vegetables should be washed.

- All fruit and vegetables should be trimmed or peeled unless the recipe states otherwise.

- Salt: Maldon sea salt undoubtedly has the best flavour, without bitterness or sharpness. For this reason I think it best to use Maldon, or another sea salt, for seasoning a dish. If you also use free-running table salt in your kitchen, restrict its use to salting boiling water and reserve your Maldon for seasoning the dish.

SOUPS AND LIGHT MEALS

tuscan bean and rosemary soup

This is a typical staple dish from Italy – a long, slow-cooked hearty broth that can sustain until the next meal, or be the first of several courses. To serve it as the Italians would, place some crusty bread in the bottom of individual bowls and ladle the soup over. This provides a substantial warming dish that makes clever use of day-old bread.

serves **6** • prep time **15 mins** • cooking time **4 hours on high/8 hours on low**

4 garlic cloves, peeled
8 tbsp roughly chopped rosemary
6 tbsp olive oil
2 celery sticks, chopped
2 carrots, chopped
2 onions, chopped
2 litres vegetable stock

3 x 400 g cans haricot beans, rinsed and drained
½ Savoy cabbage or 2 heads of greens, finely sliced
Salt and freshly ground black pepper
4 tbsp extra virgin olive oil, to serve

1 Place the garlic, rosemary and a large pinch of salt on a chopping board and chop until fine. Using the flat of the blade, crush to release the rosemary oils.

2 Heat the olive oil in a large frying pan over a medium heat and cook the celery, carrots, onions, garlic and rosemary, along with plenty of freshly ground pepper, for 10 minutes, until softened.

3 Transfer to the slow cooker and pour in the stock and beans.

4 Cook for 4 hours on the high setting or 8 hours on low, adding the cabbage or greens for the last 20 minutes of cooking. If you are using the holding feature on the slow cooker, cook the cabbage in a separate pan and stir in just before serving. Serve in individual bowls drizzled with extra virgin olive oil.

butternut squash and chorizo soup

Warming, rich and satisfying, this is a heartwarming soup to welcome you home on an autumn day. When in season, the butternut squash can easily be replaced with pumpkin, which gives a creamy finish to the soup.

serves **6** • prep time **15 mins** • cooking time **4 hours on high/8 hours on low**

1 kg butternut squash, deseeded
4 red Romero peppers or 3 ordinary
  red peppers, deseeded
4 tbsp olive oil
2 celery sticks, roughly chopped
2 onions, roughly chopped
2 garlic cloves, finely chopped
400 g potato, chopped

2 tsp dried oregano
2 tsp sweet paprika
Pinch chilli flakes
1 tbsp sherry vinegar, plus extra to serve
  (optional)
1 litre vegetable stock
75 g chorizo
Salt and freshly ground black pepper

1   Roughly chop the squash and peppers, reserving a quarter of the pepper and about 75 g of the squash. Heat 3 tablespoons of the olive oil over a medium heat in a large pan. Add the squash, peppers, celery, onions, garlic and potato and leave to soften, loosely covered, for 10 minutes.

2   Add the oregano, paprika, chilli flakes, sherry vinegar (if using) and stock. Add seasoning and bring to the boil. Place in the slow cooker and cook for 4 hours on the high setting or 8 hours on low.

3   About 15 minutes before the end of the cooking time, chop the reserved pepper, squash and chorizo into small pieces. If you prefer a smooth soup, blend the mixture with a hand blender (far safer than using a food processor).

4   Heat a small frying pan, add the chorizo and vegetables and cook for 10 minutes, over a medium heat, stirring until the squash is golden.

5   To serve, check the seasoning and serve topped with the chorizo and vegetable garnish and an extra drizzle of sherry vinegar.

corn chowder

When they are in season, corn cobs are full of sweet flavour and goodness. As they are cheap and widely available, and also stand up well to the long cooking time, they are a slow cook's ideal ingredient.

serves **6** • prep time **15 mins** • cooking time **4 hours on high/8 hours on low**

60 g butter
2 onions, chopped
1 red pepper, deseeded and chopped
4 rashers streaky bacon, chopped
4 corn cobs

4 new potatoes, diced
2 beef tomatoes, chopped
1 litre chicken stock
300 ml double cream
Salt and freshly ground black pepper

1   Heat the butter in a frying pan over a medium heat, and cook the onions, red pepper and bacon together. Season with pepper and transfer to the slow cooker.

2   Hold the cobs, one at a time, inside a clean plastic bag. Take a sharp knife and run it straight down between the rows of corn, cutting away from you. The kernels will collect in the bag rather than flying all over your kitchen.

3   Add the corn to the slow cooker, and stir in the potatoes, tomatoes and chicken stock. Check the seasoning and then leave to cook for 4 hours on the high setting or 8 hours on low.

4   About 10 minutes before the end of the cooking time, stir in the double cream. Serve hot.

leek and potato soup

This velvety soup is a traditional combination, comforting in the familiarity of its simple flavours. Serve it midweek for a working lunch, or on Saturday evening to your dinner guests. I also enjoy eating it cold in the summer, with a dash of cream and some white pepper – British food at its best!

serves **6** • prep time **15 mins** • cooking time **4 hours on high/8 hours on low**

2 tbsp sunflower oil
30 g butter
4 leeks, chopped
1.5 litres chicken stock
2 bay leaves

3 potatoes, diced
3 tbsp chopped flat-leaf parsley
4 rashers streaky bacon, chopped
 and fried
Salt and freshly ground white pepper

1 Heat the oil and butter in a large saucepan over a medium heat and cook the leeks for about 3 minutes, until softened, stirring often to stop them catching. Reserve a few leeks for the garnish. Add the stock, stir until hot, then transfer the mixture to the slow cooker.

2 Add the bay leaves and potatoes and season with salt and white pepper. Cook for 4 hours on the high setting or 8 hours on low.

3 If you prefer a smooth soup, blend with a hand blender or simply mash with a potato masher to break down the potatoes. Add the chopped parsley and fried bacon, and serve.

pearl barley broth with bacon and sage

When I make soups, I usually chop everything into large pieces, chuck it all in the pan, cook it up and blend – hey presto – done. However, the extra effort of finely chopping the vegetables gives this soup a lovely hearty texture and flavour. On a midweek evening and served with some white rolls, this is all you will need for supper.

serves **6–8** • prep time **15 mins** • cooking time **4 hours on high/8 hours on low**

3 tbsp sunflower oil
250 g smoked streaky bacon, chopped
2 onions, finely chopped
2 celery sticks, finely chopped
2 carrots, finely chopped
2 potatoes, finely diced
1 turnip, chopped

4 tbsp chopped sage leaves
2 bay leaves
2 litres chicken stock
150 g pearl barley, washed thoroughly
Salt and freshly ground black pepper
Fresh white rolls, to serve

1 Heat the oil in a large saucepan over a medium heat. Add the bacon, onions, celery and carrots and cook for 10 minutes, until softened.

2 Stir in the potatoes, turnip and herbs and cook for 3–4 minutes, until all is well blended and starting to soften around the edges, stirring often.

3 Season with salt and pepper and then transfer to the slow cooker. Add the chicken stock and pearl barley and cook for 4 hours on the high setting or 8 hours on low.

4 Serve in individual warmed bowls with fresh white rolls.

morrocan chickpea soup

This is a low-fat soup that is packed with goodness, while still tasty. It is good for a British summer – when gazpacho is just too cold, but a heavier soup is not right either.

serves **6** • prep time **15 mins** • cooking time **4 hours on high/8 hours on low**

2 tbsp olive oil
2 mild onions, roughly chopped
2 garlic cloves, crushed
2 carrots, roughly chopped
1 tsp paprika
1 tbsp cumin seeds
1 red pepper, roughly chopped

800 ml vegetable stock
2 x 400 g cans chopped tomatoes
2 x 420 g cans chickpeas, drained
  and rinsed
Salt and freshly ground black pepper
50 g mixed seeds, toasted, to serve
4 tbsp chopped coriander, to serve

1 Heat the olive oil in a frying pan over a medium heat, and cook the onions, garlic and carrots for a few minutes, until softened. Stir in the paprika and cumin and cook for a further 3 minutes or so, until the cumin smells aromatic. Transfer the mixture to the slow cooker.

2 Stir in the red pepper and add the stock, canned tomatoes and chickpeas. Season well. Cook for 4 hours on the high setting or 8 hours on low.

3 When ready to eat, take out a cup of soup and blend the remainder with a hand blender. Return the cup of soup to the cooker and give it a good stir. This gives the soup some texture, but it is, of course, optional.

4 Serve the soup garnished with the toasted seeds and coriander.

midweek chunky vegetable soup

I never make this lovely, hearty soup in small quantities – it all gets eaten, however much there is. Five o'clock hunger pangs are headed off with soup, and it's also perfect for an after-school snack, or for dinner with some crusty bread and a good hunk of cheese.

serves **6** • prep time **20 mins** • cooking time **4 hours on high/8 hours on low**

50 g butter
2 carrots, roughly chopped
1 onion, roughly chopped
2 celery sticks, roughly chopped
1 turnip, roughly chopped
1 potato, roughly chopped
1 leek, trimmed and roughly chopped

1 sweet potato, roughly chopped
1 bay leaf
2 tbsp chopped parsley
200 ml hot vegetable or chicken stock
Salt and freshly ground black pepper

1 Heat the butter in a large saucepan over a medium heat and cook the vegetables for about 5 minutes, until softened. Add seasoning and transfer everything to the slow cooker.

2 Add the bay leaf and parsley and then pour on the stock. Cook for 4 hours on the high setting or 8 hours on low.

3 When cooked, use a potato masher to mash the soup a little, leaving a rough texture. Serve hot.

celeriac and roquefort soup

It is a happy coincidence that the primitive and other-worldly-looking celeriac is at its savoury best just as the Roquefort cheese's flavour reaches its peak in December after months of ripening in the damp caves of southern France. The two marry together here in a rich soup, delicious, but quite grown up in flavour.

serves **6** • prep time **15 mins** • cooking time **4 hours on high/8 hours on low**

3 tbsp olive oil
1 kg celeriac (about 2 celeriacs),
   chopped
3 onions, chopped
500 g turnip (about 2 turnips), chopped

1.5 litres chicken stock
4 tbsp roughly chopped flat-leaf parsley
Salt and freshly ground black pepper
200 g Roquefort

1 Heat the oil in a large saucepan over a medium heat. Add the celeriac, onions and turnip and cook for about 10 minutes, until starting to soften. Season and transfer to the slow cooker.

2 Pour in the hot stock and cook for 4 hours on the high setting or 8 hours on low.

3 Sprinkle on the parsley and blend until smooth, using a hand blender, or mash by hand with a masher. Although it will not be so smooth using the latter, the resulting soup is still just as tasty. Ladle into individual bowls, crumble the Roquefort over the top of each and serve immediately.

fresh tomato and basil soup

I never need an excuse to buy tomatoes when they are sweetest, in the summer months, but if I did, it would be for the wonderful smell they release when sizzling in a pan with olive oil and garlic. This soup makes me crave crusty bread and oil to dip it in, followed by a crunchy salad and grilled meats.

serves **6** • prep time **15 mins** • cooking time **4 hours on high/8 hours on low**

6 tbsp olive oil
8 shallots, chopped
1 kg very ripe tomatoes, sliced
2 garlic cloves, crushed
300 ml vegetable stock

Salt and freshly ground black pepper
30 g basil leaves, torn, to serve
30 g butter, to serve
Thin slices of baguette, toasted, to serve

1 Gently heat half the olive oil in a frying pan and add the shallots. Cook for 5 minutes over a medium heat to soften and then transfer to the slow cooker.

2 Heat the remaining oil and cook the tomatoes over a medium heat for about 3 minutes, stirring often, until softened and broken down slightly, then stir in the garlic and cook for about a further 3 minutes, until it is all deliciously aromatic, and the tomatoes smell sweet and pungent. Season well and spoon into the slow cooker.

3 Pour on the vegetable stock – you might need more or less than specified in the ingredients, depending on how watery the tomatoes are. Cook for 4 hours on the high setting or 8 hours on low.

4 To serve, stir in the basil and butter and put a slice of bread in the base of each bowl before spooning the soup over the top.

spicy noodle soup

I have not mastered the oriental art of eating soup noodles with chopsticks – I cut mine up with scissors, so they don't fall off the spoon! I leave the choice up to you, although you might prefer to practise with chopsticks when alone, as it can be messy.

serves **6** • prep time **15 mins** • cooking time **4 hours on high/8 hours on low**

2 tbsp groundnut oil
3 garlic cloves, chopped
2 red chillies, deseeded and sliced
4 cm piece fresh root ginger, grated
2 onions, chopped
2 carrots, chopped
750 g chicken, diced

2 litres chicken stock
1 tbsp sesame oil
375 g fine egg noodles
Salt
30 g coriander leaves, chopped, to garnish
6 spring onions, chopped, to garnish

1 Heat the groundnut oil over a high heat in a large saucepan and add the garlic, chillies, ginger, onions and carrots. Cook for about 2 minutes, until softened.

2 Add the chicken and cook for about 3 minutes, stirring occasionally, until sealed. Spoon all the ingredients into the slow cooker and then pour over the hot stock and sesame oil. Add some salt for seasoning.

3 Cook on a high setting for 4 hours, or on a low setting for 8 hours. About 15 minutes before the end of the cooking time, add the noodles to the slow cooker.

4 To serve, ladle into individual bowls, chop the noodles with scissors (if desired) and sprinkle over the coriander leaves and spring onions.

thai chicken soup

For a quick and easy midweek supper, make this soup in the morning and on the way home pick up some Thai spring rolls to serve with it.

serves **6** • prep time **15 mins** • cooking time **4 hours on high/8 hours on low**

2 tbsp groundnut oil
3 garlic cloves, chopped
4 cm fresh root ginger, grated
2 onions, chopped
2 carrots, finely sliced
1 lemongrass stalk, finely chopped
2 red chillies, sliced
4 kaffir lime leaves

750 g chicken, finely diced
2 litres chicken stock
3 tbsp fish sauce
2 tbsp tamarind paste
Cellophane rice noodles
Handful coriander leaves, to serve
3 limes, cut into quarters
Soy sauce, to serve

1 Heat half the groundnut oil in a large saucepan over a high heat and add the garlic, ginger, onions and carrots. Cook for 1 minute and transfer to the slow cooker. Stir in the lemongrass, chillies and kaffir lime leaves.

2 Heat the remaining oil over a high heat in the saucepan and cook the chicken until it is sealed all over. Spoon the chicken into the slow cooker. Pour over the stock and stir in the fish sauce and tamarind paste.

3 Cook for 4 hours on the high setting or 8 hours on low. About 15 minutes before the end of the cooking time, add the noodles to the soup.

4 Serve in large bowls, sprinkled with the coriander, and hand the lime quarters and soy sauce around separately. A cup is perfect for serving the broth but you might find it easier to use tongs for transferring the noodles.

vietnamese pork and noodle soup

I love this soup. The freshness of the mint, lime and red chilli awaken the palate and lead you into a flavoursome and light broth, full of texture and exuding goodness and warmth.

serves **6** • prep time **15 mins** • cooking time **4 hours on high/8 hours on low**

300 g pork mince
2 spring onions, chopped
2 garlic cloves, chopped
1 lemongrass stalk, outer stems
    removed, finely chopped
1 egg white
1 tbsp cornflour
2 tbsp sunflower oil
3 shallots, quartered
2 carrots, finely sliced
5 cm piece fresh root ginger,
    thinly sliced

1 star anise
1 cinnamon stick
900 ml chicken stock
100 ml fish sauce
400 g flat rice noodles or rice sticks
Salt and freshly ground black pepper
2 red chillies, deseeded and finely
    chopped, to serve
2 limes, quartered, to serve
50 g mint leaves, to serve
50 g coriander leaves, to serve

1   Mix together the pork mince, spring onions, garlic, lemongrass, egg white and cornflour. Season.

2   Heat the oil in a frying panover a high heat. Add teaspoonfuls of the meat mixture and fry for about a minute to seal all over. The mix will make approximately 40 tiny meatballs. Spoon them into the slow cooker.

3   Add the shallots, carrots, ginger, star anise, cinnamon stick, stock and fish sauce to the slow cooker and gently mix together. Cook for 4 hours on the high setting or 8 hours on low.

4   About 15 minutes before the end of the cooking time, add the noodles or rice sticks to the soup. When they are cooked, but still firm, remove the cinnamon stick and ginger root, and serve with the chillies, limes, mint and coriander.

spiced tomato soup

This spicy soup is made using a combination of fresh and canned tomatoes. When in season you could use all fresh, ripe fruits as this is when tomatoes are at their sweetest and most flavoursome, making this a truly spectacular soup.

serves **6** • prep time **15 mins** • cooking time **4 hours on high/8 hours on low**

6 tbsp sunflower oil
2 onions, chopped
3 carrots, chopped
2 garlic cloves, crushed
500 g very ripe tomatoes, chopped
1 tbsp paprika
1 tbsp coriander seeds, crushed
1 tbsp cumin seeds, crushed

1 tsp granulated or caster sugar
800 g canned tomatoes, chopped
300 ml hot vegetable stock
3 tbsp chopped coriander
Poppadoms, to serve
Sea salt and freshly ground
   black pepper

1   Heat half the oil in a large pan over a high heat and cook the onions, carrots and garlic for 5 minutes. Transfer to the slow cooker.

2   Heat the remaining oil in a clean pan and cook the fresh tomatoes with the paprika and the crushed coriander and cumin seeds over a medium heat for 3 minutes until it is all deliciously aromatic. Season well, then transfer to the slow cooker with the sugar.

3   Pour over the canned tomatoes and stock (you may not need all of the stock, depending on how watery the tomatoes are), then cook for 4 hours on the high setting or 8 hours on low.

4   Serve garnished with the coriander and with the poppadoms alongside.

tomato and lentil soup

A delicious twist on a classic recipe; this tasty and satisfying soup is easy to make with storecupboard ingredients. It will soon become a favourite standby; make a large quantity and you can freeze it in batches. Serve it hot with fresh crusty bread.

serves **6** • prep time **15 mins** • cooking time **4 hours on high/8 hours on low**

3 tbsp olive oil
2 onions, chopped
3 carrots, peeled and chopped
1 potato, peeled and chopped
1 bay leaf
Pinch of paprika

2 litres hot vegetable stock
2 tbsp tomato purée
500 g tomato passata
150 g red lentils
Salt and freshly ground black pepper

1 Heat the oil in a large pan over a medium heat and cook the onions, carrots and potato for 5 minutes. Transfer to the slow cooker.

2 Stir in the bay leaf and paprika, then add the stock, tomato purée, passata and lentils. Season well and cook for 4 hours on the high setting or 8 hours on low.

creamy pumpkin and lentil soup

A deliciously autumnal soup is all you need when the rain is lashing down outside and you want to warm the cockles. The addition of lentils to this hearty dish means you can simply serve some warm crusty bread alongside it to make a satisfying meal.

serves **6** • prep time **20 mins** • cooking time **4 hours on high/8 hours on low**

3 tbsp olive oil
1 kg pumpkin, peeled, seeded and
   roughly chopped
2 celery sticks, roughly chopped
2 large onions, roughly chopped
2 carrots, roughly chopped
2 garlic cloves, finely chopped

1 bay leaf
150 g red lentils
2 litres hot vegetable stock
3 tbsp crème fraîche
2 tsp sweet paprika
Salt and freshly ground black pepper

1 Heat the oil in a large pan and cook the pumpkin, celery, onions, carrots and garlic over a high heat for 10 minutes. Transfer to the slow cooker.

2 Add the bay leaf, lentils and the stock. Season well and cook for 4 hours on the high setting or 8 hours on low.

3 If you prefer a smooth soup, blend with a hand blender at this point. Check the seasoning and serve garnished with spoonfuls of crème fraîche and the paprika sprinkled over.

spiced parsnip soup

This warming wintry soup is a perennial favourite. Parsnip is a delicious and economical vegetable with a richness and full flavour that responds well to Indian spices. For an authentic touch, serve this with mini poppadoms and a bowl of cool raita alongside.

serves **6** • prep time **10 mins** • cooking time **4 hours on high/8 hours on low**

2 tbsp sunflower oil
30 g butter
2 onions, roughly chopped
1 kg parsnips, peeled and
  roughly chopped
2 garlic cloves, crushed
2 tbsp medium curry powder

1 tsp paprika (optional)
400 g can butter beans, drained
  and rinsed
1 litre hot vegetable stock
4 tbsp chopped coriander, to serve
Salt and freshly ground black pepper

1 Heat the oil and butter in a large pan and cook the onions, parsnips and garlic over a medium heat for about 5 minutes until soft. Stir in the curry powder and paprika (if using) and transfer the mixture to the slow cooker.

2 Add the beans and the stock. Season well, bring to the boil and cook for 4 hours on the high setting or 8 hours on low.

3 Blend the soup with a hand blender until smooth, check the seasoning and serve sprinkled with coriander.

hearty bean broth with herbs

Made from storecupboard ingredients, this is the perfect soup for lazy weekends when you can't face heading out to the shops. The beans hold up really well over the lengthy cooking time, so mash a few at the end to add a richness and silkiness to the texture.

serves **6** • prep time **15 mins** • cooking time **4 hours on high/8 hours on low**

50 g butter
2 celery sticks, chopped
3 carrots, chopped
2 onions, chopped
1 potato, peeled and roughly chopped
2 litres hot light vegetable stock
1 bay leaf
1 tbsp fresh or dried thyme

2 x 400 g cans haricot beans, drained and rinsed
2 x 400 g cans flageolet beans, drained and rinsed
500 g creamed tomatoes or passata
3 tbsp finely chopped flat-leaf parsley
Sea salt and freshly ground black pepper

1 Heat the butter in a large pan over a medium heat and lightly brown the celery, carrots and onions for 10 minutes.

2 Transfer to the slow cooker and add the potato along with the stock, bay leaf, thyme, beans and creamed tomatoes or passata. Season well then cook for 4 hours on the high setting or 8 hours on low.

3 Remove the bay leaf then take out 500 ml of the soup and blend it until smooth. Return the purée to the rest of the soup in the slow cooker and stir to blend it in. Alternatively, remove 500 ml of the soup and, using a potato masher, lightly crush the beans and return the mixture to the soup. Stir in the parsley, and serve.

creamy cauliflower and chickpea soup

This smooth soup is packed with goodness, despite the decadent inclusion of cream. Ideal for a sophisticated starter, or serve as a comforting lunch with warm crusty bread.

serves **6** • prep time **15 mins** • cooking time **4 hours on high/8 hours on low**

30 g butter
3 onions, chopped
1 carrot, chopped
1 cauliflower, chopped
400 g can chickpeas, drained and rinsed

500 ml hot vegetable stock
1 bay leaf
100 ml double cream
Salt and freshly ground black pepper

1   Heat the butter in a large pan over a medium heat and cook the onions and carrot for 5 minutes until softened. Transfer to the slow cooker.

2   Add the cauliflower, then the chickpeas and pour over the stock. Season well, add the bay leaf and cook for 4 hours on the high setting or 8 hours on low.

3   At the end of the cooking time, remove the bay leaf and blend the soup using a hand blender until smooth and creamy. Add cream to taste, check the seasoning, then serve immediately.

spicy tom yam thai soup

I love this spicy soup; it's guaranteed to lift the spirits and cheer you up if you're feeling under the weather. Serve it piping hot over noodles for a delicious taste sensation.

serves **6** • prep time **15 mins** • cooking time **4 hours on high/8 hours on low**

2 tbsp groundnut oil
2 onions, chopped
2 carrots, finely sliced
1 lemongrass stalk, finely chopped
2 tbsp red Thai curry paste
4 kaffir lime leaves (optional)
750 g boneless, skinless chicken breasts
   or thighs, finely diced

2 litres hot chicken stock
3 tbsp fish sauce
Cellophane rice noodles, to serve
3 spring onions, finely sliced, to serve
3 limes, quartered, to serve
Soy sauce, to serve

1   Heat half the oil in a large pan over a high heat and add the onions and carrots. Cook for 1 minute then transfer to the slow cooker. Add the lemongrass, Thai curry paste and lime leaves, if using, to the vegetables.

2   Heat the remaining oil in a large pan and cook the chicken until it is sealed all over, then transfer to the slow cooker. Pour over the stock and the fish sauce and cook for 4 hours on the high setting or 8 hours on low.

3   About 15 minutes before the end of the cooking time, add the noodles to the soup.

4   Spoon the hot soup into large bowls and sprinkle with the spring onions. (You may find it easier to use tongs to fish out the noodles, and if you prefer, a large cup is perfect to serve the broth in.) Serve with the lime quarters and the soy sauce offered separately.

chicken pot pie soup

This soup is a fantastic all-in-one lunch dish that was made famous by a London lunch bar called 'EAT'. It is just filling enough, and just warming enough not to make you sleepy for the afternoon shift.

serves **6** • prep time **15 mins** • cooking time **4 hours on high/8 hours on low**

2 tbsp sunflower oil
30 g butter
2 leeks, chopped
2 carrots, chopped
500 g boneless, skinless chicken breasts
   or thighs, finely diced
2 tbsp plain flour
300 ml hot chicken stock

300 ml milk
1 bay leaf
500 g pack ready-rolled puff pastry
1 beaten egg
100 g peas, fresh or frozen
3 tbsp finely chopped flat-leaf parsley,
Salt and freshly ground black pepper

1 Heat half the oil with all the butter in a large frying pan over a medium heat and cook the leeks and carrots for 2 minutes. Transfer everything to the slow cooker.

2 Heat the remaining oil in the frying pan over a high heat and cook the chicken until it is sealed all over. Spoon the chicken into the slow cooker and stir in the flour. Pour over the stock and milk and season well. Add the bay leaf and cook for 4 hours on the high setting or 8 hours on low.

3 To make the puff pastry 'lids', first preheat the oven to 200°C/Gas 6. Cut out 6 puff pastry rounds, each 6 cm in diameter, place them on a baking sheet and brush each with a little beaten egg. Bake in the hot oven for 10 minutes or until puffed and golden. Set aside until ready to serve. (If you are making the soup and freezing it, the uncooked pastry rounds can be frozen then baked straight from the freezer at the same temperature – simply add 5 minutes to the cooking time.)

4 About 15 minutes before the end of the cooking time, stir the peas and parsley into the soup. Serve hot in bowls topped with a puff pastry round.

sweet potato and chicken soup

This soup is the perfect revitalising all-in-one meal. I like to make it in large quantities then freeze it in portions to defrost and reheat to take to work, or for a simple supper to greet me at the end of a long day.

serves **6** • prep time **15 mins** • cooking time **4 hours on high/8 hours on low**

2 tbsp sunflower oil
30 g butter
1 leek, chopped
2 celery sticks, chopped
Few sage leaves, chopped (optional)
300 g boneless, skinless chicken
  thighs, diced

2 bay leaves
2 medium sweet potatoes, about 350 g,
  peeled and diced
1.5 litres hot chicken stock
Extra virgin olive oil, to serve
Salt and freshly ground black pepper

1   Heat the oil and butter in a large pan over a medium heat and cook the leek, celery, sage (if using) and chicken for about 3 minutes until the leeks are soft, stirring often to prevent them catching. Transfer all the ingredients to the slow cooker.

2   Add the bay leaves and sweet potatoes then pour in the stock. Season well and cook for 4 hours on the high setting or 8 hours on low.

3   If you prefer a smooth soup, blend with a hand blender at this point. (I never recommend blending hot soup in the food processor; I think it is far safer to use a stick blender in the pan.) Otherwise, simply mash with a potato masher to break down the potatoes.

4   Serve hot drizzled with extra virgin olive oil.

hungarian beef goulash soup

The ultimate meal in a bowl. This is a soupy take on the classic beef casserole dish, which makes a substantial snack or a hearty dinner for a cold day.

serves **6** • prep time **15 mins** • cooking time **4 hours on high/8 hours on low**

2 tbsp oil
30 g butter
2 onions, chopped
2 red peppers, chopped
2 green peppers, chopped
400 g beef, finely diced
1 tbsp paprika
2 tbsp tomato purée

300 ml hot beef stock
200 g tomato passata
400 g can pinto beans, drained
   and rinsed
3 tbsp finely chopped dill
6 tsp crème fraîche, to serve
Salt and freshly ground black pepper

1 Heat the oil and butter in a large frying pan over a medium heat and add the onions and peppers. Cook for 2 minutes then transfer everything to the slow cooker.

2 Add the beef, paprika, tomato purée, stock, passata and beans to the vegetables and season well. Cook for 4 hours on a high setting or 8 hours on low.

3 About 15 minutes before the end of the cooking time, stir in the dill. If you prefer a smooth soup, blend with a hand blender at this point, or serve the soup unblended, if you like a chunky texture. Serve each bowl of soup topped with a blob of crème fraîche.

mediterranean swordfish and olive stew

This tasty dish has all the flavours of the Mediterranean; one mouthful will transport you there in an instant. This low-fat, full-flavoured stew makes an easy, light midweek supper or a simple yet impressive dinner-party dish.

serves **4** • prep time **15 mins** • cooking time **4 hours on high/8 hours on low**

2 tbsp olive oil
2 onions, chopped
1 carrot, chopped
1 red pepper, chopped
3 garlic cloves, crushed
1 tbsp fennel seeds
400 g can chopped tomatoes

4 x 150 g swordfish steaks
200 ml white wine
Grated zest of 1 lemon
4 tbsp finely chopped flat-leaf parsley
100 g black olives, pitted and chopped
Sea salt and freshly ground
 black pepper

1 Heat half the oil in a medium frying pan over a medium heat and cook the onions, carrot, pepper and garlic for 2 minutes until soft. Transfer to the slow cooker and stir in the fennel seeds and tomatoes.

2 Heat the remaining oil in a large clean frying pan over a high heat. Season the swordfish steaks and cook them for 1 minute on each side. Add the cooked fish to the slow cooker.

3 Add the wine to the hot frying pan, simmer for a couple of minutes to burn off the alcohol, then pour the liquid into the slow cooker. Cook the stew for 4 hours on the high setting or 8 hours on low.

4 Mix together the lemon zest, parsley and black olives and sprinkle over the stew to serve.

chilli thai-style squid

Squid is a really economical seafood, and slow-cooking it brings out all its delicious flavours. A popular Mediterranean and Eastern ingredient, squid is the perfect partner to all kinds of spices, and its natural richness means it needs little else to make this a simple yet satisfying curry.

serves **6** • prep time **20 mins** • cooking time **4 hours on high/8 hours on low**

3 tbsp vegetable or olive oil
1 kg frozen squid, diced
4 spring onions, sliced
3 garlic cloves, sliced
2 carrots, sliced
90 g red Thai curry paste
3 tbsp Thai fish sauce
440 ml coconut milk

2 tbsp soy sauce
1 red pepper, chopped
6 tbsp fresh lime juice
2 tbsp finely chopped coriander leaves
2 tbsp finely chopped basil leaves
1 red chilli, seeded and finely sliced
Thai jasmine rice, to serve

1 Heat the oil in a frying pan over a high heat and cook the squid, spring onions, garlic and carrots for 2 minutes until lightly browned. Transfer to the slow cooker.

2 In the frying pan, combine the curry paste with the fish sauce, coconut milk and soy sauce. Heat to a simmer and pour over the squid. Add the red pepper to the curry and cook for 4 hours on the high setting or 8 hours on low.

3 Just before serving, cook the rice according to the packet instructions.

4 Add the lime juice, coriander, basil and chilli to the curry, mix it in well and serve in large bowls with the rice.

squid pilaf with parsley and garlic

You can buy squid ready-prepared in most supermarkets, but if you're lucky enough to have a fishmonger near you, ask him to cut up a fresh squid for you. Squid can be quite rich, but in this recipe its flavour is kept fresh with the addition of spring onions.

serves **6** • prep time **15 mins** • cooking time **3 hours on high/6 hours on low**

2 tbsp olive oil
400 g squid tubes, sliced into rings
1 large mild onion, chopped
2 carrots, chopped
1 bay leaf
2 tsp coriander seeds, crushed
1 tsp chilli flakes
3 garlic cloves, chopped

200 g brown rice, washed
200 g puy lentils, washed
1 litre hot fish stock
50 g flat-leaf parsley, chopped
6 spring onions, finely sliced
Rocket salad, to serve
Salt and freshly ground black pepper

1 Heat the oil in a large frying pan over a medium heat. Add the squid rings, onion and carrots and fry for a couple of minutes until golden. Transfer to the slow cooker.

2 Add the bay leaf, coriander seeds, chilli flakes and garlic and fry gently until the spices are aromatic.

3 Stir in the rice and lentils, pour on the stock and cook for 3 hours on the high setting or 6 hours on low.

4 Just before serving, stir through the parsley and spring onions. Serve hot with the rocket salad.

seafood risotto

You may find your local supermarket or deli has a variety of risotto rices on offer, including the most commonly available Arborio and Carnaroli varieties. However, for slow cooking I would recommend using the equally widely sold *Vialone nano*, because even after lengthy cooking it keeps some texture and the essential 'bite' that is needed for the perfect risotto.

serves **6** • prep time **15 mins** • cooking time **4 hours on high/8 hours on low**

2 tbsp olive oil
2 onions, chopped
3 garlic cloves, chopped
500 g vialone nano risotto rice
1 bay leaf
1 tsp paprika
250 ml white wine

1 litre hot fish stock
500 ml shellfish soup
400 g frozen seafood, defrosted
100 g grated Parmesan
12 cherry tomatoes, halved
Salt and freshly ground black pepper

1   Heat the oil in a large pan over a medium heat and cook the onions and garlic for about 10 minutes until soft but not coloured.

2   Add the rice, bay leaf, paprika and wine and cook for a few minutes to heat it all through.

3   Transfer everything to the slow cooker and add the stock, shellfish soup and seafood. Season well and cook for 4 hours on the high setting or 8 hours on low.

4   Stir through the Parmesan and the cherry tomatoes before serving.

crayfish pilaf with fresh rocket salsa

Crayfish are now widely available in the freezer cabinet of most super-markets, and their meaty succulence makes a nice change from prawns and other shellfish traditionally used in pilaf. This recipe uses brown rice in combination with spelt grain, which is a healthy wholegrain with a low gluten content, so it's good to serve to someone who is gluten intolerant.

serves **6** • prep time **15 mins** • cooking time **3 hours on high/6 hours on low**

3 tbsp olive oil
1 large mild onion, chopped
3 garlic cloves, chopped
1 bay leaf
150 g brown rice, washed
150 g spelt grain, washed
1.2 litres hot fish stock
300 g raw king prawns, peeled
350 g frozen cooked crayfish, defrosted
  and halved

85 g bag rocket and watercress salad
2 tbsp flat-leaf parsley
3 spring onions, finely sliced
2 tomatoes, chopped
1 fresh red chilli, seeded and finely
  chopped (optional)
Sea salt and freshly ground
  black pepper

1 Heat 2 tablespoons of the oil in a large frying pan over a medium heat. Add the onion and garlic and fry for 3–4 minutes until the onion is softened. Stir in the bay leaf, rice and spelt and mix to coat in the oil. Transfer everything to the slow cooker.

2 Pour over the stock and stir in the prawns. Cook for 3 hours on the high setting or 6 hours on low.

3 About 30 minutes before the end of the cooking time, stir in the crayfish.

4 To make the salsa, blend together the rocket salad, parsley, spring onions, tomatoes, chilli (if using) and remaining oil in a food processor or blender until finely chopped. Season well.

5 Serve the crayfish pilaf with the rocket salsa on the side.

tuna baked with artichokes and capers

This is one of my favourite dishes, and one I can eat all year round as many of the ingredients are good storecupboard standbys. Fish and capers are a classic combination, and here mildly flavoured tuna is given a real lift from the slightly bitter artichokes and salty capers. For the best result, cook on high for the shorter time.

serves **4** • prep time**15 mins** • cooking time **4 hours on high/8 hours on low**

2 tbsp olive oil
4 tuna steaks, approx. 125 g each
3 garlic cloves, crushed
Grated zest of 1 lemon
2 tbsp salted capers, drained and rinsed

4 tbsp finely chopped flat-leaf parsley
200 ml white wine
100 ml hot fish stock
280 g jar artichokes in oil, drained
Salt and freshly ground black pepper

1 Heat the oil in a large frying pan over a high heat and fry the tuna steaks for about a minute on each side until golden. Transfer to the slow cooker.

2 Add the garlic, lemon zest, capers and parsley to the slow cooker. Pour over the wine and stock and season well. Cook for 4 hours on the high setting or 8 hours on low.

3 About 15 minutes before the end of the cooking time, add the artichokes. Serve piping hot.

tuna and spinach hotpot

Some light meals can leave those with a hearty appetite still feeling hungry, however tuna steaks are always satisfying – even for the most committed carnivore! If you're not confident at cooking tuna, slow cooking is the answer, as you are not at risk of overcooking the fish and leaving it dry. Make sure the pan is quite hot before you add the tuna so that the golden crust forms quickly. Serve with hot boiled new potatoes.

serves **4** • prep time **15 mins** • cooking time **4 hours on high/8 hours on low**

2 tbsp olive oil
4 x 150 g tuna steaks
2 garlic cloves, crushed
400 g can chopped tomatoes
100 ml white wine
200 g spinach leaves, washed and
  roughly chopped

4 tbsp finely chopped flat-leaf parsley
  to serve
Sea salt and freshly ground
  black pepper

1 Heat the oil in a large frying pan over a high heat. Season the tuna steaks and cook for 3 minutes or until golden. Add the garlic for the last minute. Transfer everything to the slow cooker, with all the pan juices.

2 Add the tomatoes and wine to the slow cooker and season well, then cook for 4 hours on the high setting or 8 hours on low.

3 About 10 minutes before the end of the cooking time, stir in the spinach leaves. Serve garnished with the parsley.

chicken with beans, hazelnuts and orange

I love to add lots of texture and flavour to a dish in place of richness. Crunchy hazelnuts, tangy oranges and succulent green beans make this a tasty dish.

serves **6** • prep time **15 mins** • cooking time **4 hours on high/8 hours on low**

1.5 kg chicken pieces, skin removed
2 tbsp olive oil
1 tbsp plain flour
6 shallots, roughly sliced
3 garlic cloves, chopped
50 g hazelnuts, halved

100 ml hot chicken stock
100 ml fresh orange juice
200 g green beans, halved
4 tbsp chopped flat-leaf parsley
1 kg new potatoes, to serve
Salt and freshly ground black pepper

1 Season the chicken. Heat half the oil in a large frying pan over a medium heat and fry the chicken until golden all over. Spoon into the slow cooker and stir in the flour.

2 Heat the remaining oil in the frying pan and soften the shallots and garlic. Add to the slow cooker with the hazelnuts, stock and orange juice and cook for 4 hours on the high setting or 8 hours on low.

3 About 30 minutes before the end of cooking time, add the beans and stir in the parsley.

4 Towards the end of the cooking time, cook the new potatoes over a high heat in a pan of lightly salted boiling water until tender. Serve immediately with the chicken and sauce.

chicken with sweet and sour noodles

This is a great dish for all the family, and a particular favourite of hungry children returning from school. For a more substantial meal, serve it with spring rolls and sesame toasts.

serves **6** • prep time **15 mins** • cooking time **4 hours on high/8 hours on low**

900 g boneless skinless chicken thighs
2 tbsp cornflour
4 tbsp soy sauce
4 tbsp granulated or caster sugar
100 ml garlic vinegar
6 tbsp tomato purée
100 ml orange juice
225 g can pineapple in natural juice
200 ml hot chicken stock

2 tbsp groundnut oil
2 onions, sliced
1 red pepper, roughly chopped
1 green pepper, roughly chopped
2 carrots, sliced
Rice noodles, to serve
Salt and freshly ground black pepper

1 Season the chicken and toss it in the cornflour to coat.

2 In a bowl, mix together the soy sauce, sugar, vinegar, tomato purée, orange juice, pineapple and stock and pour everything into the slow cooker.

3 Heat the oil in a large frying pan over a medium heat and cook the onions, peppers and carrots for 2 minutes. When just golden, transfer to the slow cooker. Season.

4 Add the chicken to the other ingredients in the slow cooker and cook for 4 hours on the high setting or 8 hours on low.

5 About 15 minutes before serving, cook the rice noodles: drop the noodles into a large pan of boiling water, and when it returns to the boil, add a cup of cold water. Repeat this, then when the water boils for the third time, drain the noodles, which will be cooked perfectly.

6 Scoop out the cooked chicken from the slow cooker and serve with the noodles stirred into the sweet and sour sauce.

chicken with artichokes and pink peppercorns

This may not seem an obvious combination of ingredients, but pink peppercorns have a fragrant flavour and a lovely texture that marry surprisingly well with slightly bitter artichokes. Serve with fresh pasta for a delicious and impressive dinner-party dish.

serves **6** • prep time **15 mins** • cooking time **4 hours on high/8 hours on low**

1.5 kg chicken pieces, skin removed
2 tbsp olive oil
1 tbsp plain flour
2 mild onions, chopped
2 red peppers, chopped
4 garlic cloves, chopped
2 tbsp pink peppercorns in brine,
 drained

100 ml white wine
280 g jar artichokes in brine, drained
Tagliatelle, to serve
4 tbsp chopped flat-leaf parsley,
 to serve
Salt and freshly ground black pepper

1 Season the chicken. Heat half the oil in a large frying pan over a medium heat and fry the chicken until golden all over. Spoon into the slow cooker and stir in the flour.

2 Heat the remaining oil in the pan and soften the onions, peppers and garlic. Add to the slow cooker. Crush the peppercorns lightly and add to the slow cooker. Stir in the white wine, spoon the artichokes on top and cook for 4 hours on the high setting or 8 hours on low.

3 Towards the end of the cooking time, cook the tagliatelle according to the packet instructions. Sprinkle the parsley over before serving. Drain, then serve immediately with the chicken and sauce.

turkey meatballs with red pepper sauce

If you're not a fan of onions, this recipe is for you. Onion-free, the dish instead derives flavour from its lovely rich red pepper sauce.

serves **4** • prep time **15 mins** • cooking time **4 hours on high/8 hours on low**

400 g turkey mince
1 egg white
290 g jar red peppers in brine, drained
500 g tomato passata
2 tbsp oil
2 garlic cloves, crushed
? tsp cayenne pepper

400 g can cannellini beans, drained and
  rinsed
1 large sprig of thyme leaves, chopped
600 g spaghetti, to serve
Green salad, to serve
Salt and freshly ground black pepper

1 Season the mince and stir in the egg white to bind. Divide the mix into 12 pieces and roll in your hands to form 12 meatballs.

2 Blend the red peppers and passata together in a blender or food processor until well combined. Season.

3 Heat the oil in a large frying pan over a high heat and cook the meatballs for about 2 minutes until just brown all over. Add the garlic for the second minute then transfer everything to the slow cooker.

4 Add the blended red peppers to the slow cooker with the cayenne, beans and thyme and cook for 4 hours on the high setting or 8 hours on low.

5 Just before serving, cook the spaghetti according to the packet instructions. Drain and serve with the meatballs and sauce, with a green salad on the side.

turkey with black olives, tomatoes and basil

Turkey makes a good low-fat alternative to chicken and tastes delicious in this traditional Italian sauce of olives, tomatoes and basil. For a truly authentic meal, serve it with your favourite fresh pasta.

serves **4** • prep time **15 mins** • cooking time **4 hours on high/8 hours on low**

4 turkey breast steaks, approx.
   500 g in total
2 tbsp olive oil
2 onions, roughly chopped
1 carrot, chopped
2 garlic cloves, left whole

100 g pitted black olives, sliced
1 tbsp tomato purée
500 g tomato passata
15g basil leaves, to serve
Sea salt and freshly ground
   black pepper

1 Season the turkey steaks. Heat half the oil in a large frying pan over a high heat and brown the steaks on both sides. Transfer to the slow cooker.

2 Heat the remaining oil in the frying pan and cook the onions, carrot and garlic over a medium heat for 5 minutes. Add to the slow cooker.

3 Stir in the tomato purée, passata and seasoning and cook for 4 hours on the high setting or 8 hours on low. Garnish with basil before serving.

harissa turkey stew

This light yet satisfying dish is inspired by North African cuisine; it has a real kick thanks to the fiery and vibrant harissa paste. Plain couscous makes the perfect accompaniment to this flavoursome stew.

serves **4** • prep time **15 mins** • cooking time **4 hours on high/8 hours on low**

4 turkey breast steaks, approx.
   500 g in total
2 tbsp oil
2 red onions, roughly chopped
2 carrots, peeled and roughly chopped
4 garlic cloves, left whole
1 lemon, rinsed and roughly chopped
1 tbsp tomato purée

250 g tomato passata
1 cinnamon stick
4 tbsp chopped coriander leaves
300 g couscous, to serve
Harissa paste, to taste
Natural yoghurt, to serve
Sea salt and freshly ground
   black pepper

1 Season the turkey steaks. Heat half the oil in a large frying pan over a high heat and brown the turkey steaks on both sides. Transfer to the slow cooker.

2 Heat the remaining oil in the frying pan and cook the onions, carrots and garlic in over a medium heat for 5 minutes. Add to the slow cooker with the lemon pieces.

3 Stir in the tomato purée, passata, cinnamon and seasoning and cook for 4 hours on the high setting or 8 hours on low.

4 Just before serving, prepare the couscous according to the packet instructions. Stir the coriander into the stew and serve hot over the couscous with some harissa paste and yoghurt in separate bowls to be passed around.

EASY MIDWEEK SUPPERS

salmon in chilli miso broth

This is a great dish for January – light eating after the excesses of the festive season, but satisfying too. The wasabi paste and pickled ginger are widely available, but you might have to search a bit for the dashi miso paste. Once it is in your fridge, however, you can return to it time and again. There is a powdered version, which can be used as a substitute.

serves **6** • prep time **15 mins** • cooking time **4 hours on high/8 hours on low**

2 tbsp sunflower oil
3 cm piece fresh root ginger, grated
3 garlic cloves, chopped
2–3 red chillies, deseeded and shredded
12 spring onions, cut into 5 cm lengths
150 g French green beans, halved
1 large carrot, cut into sticks
4 tbsp dashi miso paste

1 litre boiling water
6 salmon or trout fillets, skins left on
3 heads baby pak choi
Salt
Soy sauce, to serve
Pickled ginger, to serve
Wasabi paste, to serve

1   Heat the oil in a large frying pan over a high heat. Add the ginger, garlic, chillies, spring onions, beans and carrots and cook for 2 minutes, until softened. Spoon into the slow cooker.

2   In a measuring jug, dissolve the miso paste in the boiling water. Pour some of this into the pan to deglaze, then pour it all into the slow cooker with the vegetables.

3   Season the salmon fillets with a little salt. Place a dry frying pan over a high heat until very hot. Sear the salmon fillets, flesh side down, and when they are sealed, place in the slow cooker on top of the vegetables. Cover and cook for 4 hours on the high setting or 8 hours on low.

4   About 10 minutes before the end of the cooking time, add the pak choi. Serve in shallow bowls, offering the soy sauce, pickled ginger and wasabi separately. (Note that wasabi is quite peppery, so only a tiny amount is needed.)

salmon and tamarind curry

Tamarind paste comes from the fruit of the tamarind tree, and is widely used all over India when some piquancy is needed, but without the sourness of lemon, or the all-pervading sharpness of vinegar. In this dish the tamarind paste keeps the oiliness of the salmon in check.

serves **6** • prep time **15 mins** • cooking time **4 hours on high/8 hours on low**

750 g fresh tomatoes, halved
3 waxy potatoes, sliced
6 salmon or trout fillets, skins left on
2 garlic cloves, thinly sliced
40 g piece fresh root ginger, grated
1 green chilli, deseeded and sliced
1 red chilli, deseeded and sliced
1 lemongrass stalk, bruised

1 tbsp tamarind paste
200 ml hot fish stock
2 tbsp soy sauce
4 tbsp coriander leaves
2 tbsp lime juice
1 cucumber, thinly sliced,
   to serve

1 Place the tomatoes and potatoes in the slow cooker.

2 Place a dry frying pan over a high heat until hot, then dry-fry the salmon fillets for about 2 minutes on each side, until golden. Add the garlic, ginger, chillies and the lemongrass and fry briefly, before transferring the mixture to the slow cooker, being careful not to break up the fish.

3 In a measuring jug, dissolve the tamarind paste in the fish stock. Add the soy sauce and pour over the fish. Cook for 4 hours on the high setting or 8 hours on low.

4 Stir in the coriander leaves and lime juice and serve with the cucumber.

goan fish curry with lentils

The texture and flavour of Goan curries, with their smoky, earthy, sweet leaves, is different from the typical rich and creamy curry house dish. It is light and fresh, but still satisfyingly spicy. Roti bread and pickles go very well with Goan currries, which have a lot of sauce to be mopped up.

serves **6** • prep time **15 mins** • cooking time **4 hours on high/8 hours on low**

4 tbsp sunflower oil
2 onions, sliced
2 garlic cloves, sliced
200 g green lentils
1 tbsp ground turmeric
15 fresh or 30 dried curry leaves
2 tsp palm sugar or jaggery
  (see page 40)

2 green chillies, sliced
1 litre fish stock
6 x 150 g haddock fillets, skins left on
4 tomatoes, quartered
Salt
Handful coriander leaves, to garnish
12 roti breads or chappatis, to serve
Mango and lime pickles, to serve

1 Heat half the oil over a medium heat in a frying pan and cook the onions and garlic for about 5 minutes, until softened. Stir in the lentils and then the turmeric, curry leaves, sugar and chillies. Add the stock, bring to a simmer, then transfer the mixture to the slow cooker.

2 Heat the remaining oil over a high heat in the frying pan and seal the fish on both sides. Season with salt add to the slow cooker. Cook for 4 hours on the high setting or 8 hours on low.

3 About 10 minutes before the end of the cooking time, add the tomatoes and leave to soften. Garnish with coriander and serve with rotis or chappatis and pickles.

italian fish stew with pancetta and garlic

This is a really delicious way to eat squid, that economical and often overlooked seafood. If you are lucky enough to have a fish shop near you, buy a fresh large squid and ask the fishmonger to clean it for you. Don't skimp on the crusty bread to mop up the delicious juices.

serves **4** • prep time **15 mins** • cooking time **4 hours on high/8 hours on low**

4 tbsp olive oil
100 g smoked pancetta, diced
3 garlic cloves, crushed
1 tsp chilli flakes
1 x 400 g can chopped tomatoes
300 g swordfish fillets

200 ml white wine
450 g squid tubes, cut into rings
Grated zest of 1 lemon
2 tbsp finely chopped flat-leaf parsley
Salt and freshly ground black pepper
Crusty bread, to serve

1 Heat half the oil in a frying pan over a medium heat and fry the pancetta and garlic for about 2 minutes, to soften. Stir in the chilli flakes and chopped tomatoes and heat through for about 3 minutes. Transfer to the slow cooker.

2 Heat the remaining oil over a high heat in the frying pan, season the swordfish and cook for about 1 minute on each side. Add to the contents of the slow cooker.

3 Pour the wine into the hot pan, simmer for a couple of minutes, then add to the slow cooker. Finally, add the squid and season well. Cook for 4 hours on the high setting or 8 hours on low.

4 To finish, mix together the lemon zest and parsley and sprinkle over the stew. Serve in shallow bowls or on deep plates with crusty bread.

chicken pasta sauce
with sweet potato and rosemary

Sometimes a more hearty pasta sauce is needed on a cold winter evening. This sauce has all the texture of the sweet potato and the flavour of the rosemary for the pasta to soak up. Serve with lots of freshly grated Parmesan.

serves **4** • prep time **15 mins** • cooking time **4 hours on high/8 hours on low**

400 g boneless, skinless chicken
   thighs, diced
3 tbsp olive oil
2 garlic cloves
2 tbsp finely chopped rosemary
400 g sweet potatoes, peeled
   and chopped

2 leeks, chopped
200 ml hot chicken stock
100 ml crème fraîche
300 g tagliatelle, to serve
4 tbsp finely chopped flat-leaf parsley
Salt and freshly ground black pepper

1 Season the chicken. Heat half the oil in a large frying pan over a medium heat. Fry the chicken until golden all over then transfer to the slow cooker.

2 Chop together the garlic and rosemary with a bit of salt. Heat the remaining oil in the frying pan and soften the sweet potatoes, leeks and rosemary and garlic. Transfer to the slow cooker.

3 Add the stock, season, and cook for 4 hours on the high setting or 8 hours on low.

4 Just before serving, cook the pasta according to the packet instructions and stir the crème fraîche into the sauce.

5 Serve hot spooned over the tagliatelle and garnished with the parsley.

chicken with leeks, bacon and mustard

This tasty chicken casserole is a real crowd-pleaser and so versatile. A meal for any occasion, it can welcome you home at the end of a long day, or makes a delicious hassle-free weekend lunch for friends.

serves **6** • prep time **15 mins** • cooking time **4 hours on high/8 hours on low**

2 tbsp plain flour
1.5 kg chicken pieces
4 tbsp oil
100 g streaky bacon, diced
2 leeks, finely chopped
2 bay leaves
2 tbsp wholegrain Dijon mustard

2 tsp mustard powder
300 ml hot chicken stock
Salt and freshly ground black pepper
2.5 kg Maris Piper potatoes, peeled
  and chopped
50 g butter
100 ml milk

1 Season the flour with salt and pepper, then toss the chicken pieces in the flour, coating thoroughly.

2 Heat half the oil in a large frying pan over a high heat, add the chicken and cook for about 5 minutes until browned. Transfer to the slow cooker.

3 Heat the remaining oil in the pan over a medium heat and add the bacon and leeks. Cook for about 5 minutes until softened. Stir in the bay leaves and both mustards and transfer everything to the slow cooker. Add the stock and cook for 4 hours on the high setting or 8 hours on low.

4 To make the mashed potato, 30 minutes before serving put the potatoes in a large pan with enough cold salted water to cover. Bring to the boil then cook, uncovered, for 15 minutes or until tender, then drain well. Return the potatoes to the pan with the butter and milk and season well. Mash with a potato masher for some texture, or use a potato ricer or food mill if you prefer a smoother version.

5 Serve the chicken on top of the mashed potato with the sauce poured over.

piquant chicken with red and yellow peppers

This simple supper is guaranteed to lift the spirits on a week night. To save time, I have used red peppers from a jar rather than roasting them myself. Be sure to drain them well, though, so that you only get the flavour of the peppers, not the brine.

serves **6** • prep time **15 mins** • cooking time **4 hours on high/8 hours on low**

1.5 kg chicken pieces
4 tbsp olive oil
1 tbsp plain flour
2 yellow peppers, chopped
2 onions, chopped
2 garlic cloves, crushed
2 flamed red peppers in brine, chopped

3 tbsp tomato purée
1 bay leaf
1 tbsp paprika
2 tbsp balsamic vinegar
300 g long grain rice, to serve
Salt and freshly ground black pepper

1 Season the chicken. Heat half the oil in a large frying pan over a high heat and cook the chicken until browned. Transfer to the slow cooker and stir in the flour.

2 Heat the remaining oil in the frying pan and soften the yellow peppers, onions and garlic over a medium heat for 5 minutes. Season and stir in the tomato purée, red peppers, and bay leaf. Spoon everything into the slow cooker.

3 Stir in the paprika and balsamic vinegar and cook for 4 hours on the high setting or 8 hours on low.

4 Just before serving, cook the rice according to the packet instructions. Serve the chicken spooned over the cooked rice.

chicken korma

Chicken korma is a rich and mild curry, which makes it ideal for serving as a family dinner or to a crowd of friends with varying tastes. For those who do prefer a bit of heat in their curry, serve it with a spicy condiment such as a chilli relish.

serves **6** • prep time **20 mins** • cooking time **4 hours on high/8 hours on low**

4 tbsp butter
1.8 kg chicken pieces
2 onions, sliced
4 garlic cloves, crushed
5 cm piece of fresh root ginger, finely grated
50 g korma curry paste

3 tbsp tomato purée
300 ml hot chicken stock
200 ml coconut milk
15 g coriander, chopped
350 g basmati rice, to serve
50 g flaked almonds, toasted, to serve
Salt and freshly ground black pepper

1 Heat half the butter in a large frying pan set over a high heat. Season the chicken pieces and brown them all over. You will probably have to do this in batches. Transfer to the slow cooker.

2 Heat the remaining butter in the frying pan and brown the onions over a high heat, then stir in the garlic, ginger and curry paste. Transfer to the slow cooker and add the tomato purée, stock and coconut milk, stirring well. Season and cook for 4 hours on the high setting or 8 hours on low.

3 Just before serving, cook the rice according to the packet instructions. Stir the coriander into the curry and serve piping hot over the rice, garnished with the almonds.

chicken with lemon and garlic

This simple combination is delicious as an al fresco dish. Served with a green vegetable and fried potatoes, you will be transported to a French summer with every mouthful.

serves **6** • prep time **15 mins** • cooking time **4 hours on high/8 hours on low**

6 tbsp olive oil
1.5 kg chicken pieces
3 lemons, sliced
2 onions, chopped
6 garlic cloves, halved
100 ml white wine

100 ml hot chicken stock
4 tbsp chopped flat-leaf parsley,
  to serve
Green beans, to serve
Salt and freshly ground black pepper

1 Heat half the oil in a large frying pan over a medium heat. Fry the chicken until golden all over, season well and spoon into the slow cooker.

2 Heat the remaining oil in the frying pan and cook the lemons, onions and garlic over a medium heat for 5 minutes until softened. Transfer to the slow cooker.

3 Stir in the wine and stock, season well and cook for 4 hours on the high setting or 8 hours on low. Stir in the parsley just before serving.

warming chicken casserole

Chicken is such a versatile family food and so easy to prepare. This traditional casserole will win a place in your repertoire for its simple comforting flavours. It's perfect for serving with a mound of creamy mashed potato.

serves **6** • prep time **15 mins** • cooking time **4 hours on high/8 hours on low**

1.5 kg chicken pieces
50 g butter
100 g streaky bacon, each rasher
  cut into 3
2 tbsp plain flour
2 onions, chopped

3 carrots, chopped
2 celery sticks, chopped
2 bay leaves
100 ml hot chicken stock
1 tbsp Dijon mustard
Salt and freshly ground black pepper

1 Season the chicken pieces. Heat half the butter in a large frying pan over a medium heat and brown the chicken and bacon. Transfer to the slow cooker and stir in the flour.

2 Heat the remaining butter in the frying pan and soften the onions, carrots and celery. Transfer everything to the slow cooker.

3 Add the bay leaves, stock and mustard. Season well and cook for 4 hours on the high setting or 8 hours on low.

curried duck with pineapple

Duck lends itself beautifully to fruity flavours, and in this recipe the sweetness of the pineapple is the perfect complement to the spices. Serve with a zesty lime pickle if you want a little extra zing.

serves **6** • prep time **15 mins** • cooking time **4 hours on high/8 hours on low**

6 duck legs, excess fat removed
1 tbsp oil
2 onions, chopped
3 garlic cloves, crushed
5 cm piece of fresh root ginger, grated
1 tsp cayenne pepper
1 tsp ground turmeric
1 tbsp coriander seeds, crushed
1 tbsp cumin seeds, crushed

1 tbsp tomato purée
450 g can pineapple slices in
  juice, drained
1 red chilli, seeded and chopped
100 ml hot chicken stock
350 g basmati rice, to serve
Lime pickle, to serve
Salt and freshly ground black pepper

1 Season the duck legs then fry them in a large dry frying pan over a high heat. Drain on kitchen paper then place them in the slow cooker.

2 Drain off any excess fat from the frying pan, add the oil and place over a medium heat to cook the onions, garlic and ginger together for 5 minutes until softened. Stir in the cayenne, turmeric, coriander and cumin seeds and tomato purée. Transfer to the slow cooker with the pineapple, chilli and stock. Season and cook for 4 hours on the high setting or 8 hours on low.

3 Just before serving, cook the rice according to the packet instructions. Spoon off any excess fat from the duck (you may also want to take the meat off the bone, if time allows) and serve hot with lime pickle and the rice.

spiced aromatic lamb with chickpeas, lentils and coriander

Lamb lends itself very well to long slow cooking and to flavouring with spices. It is shown off at its best here, with the mild, spicy flavours mingling while the lamb tenderises and becomes succulent. You could serve it with a chilli relish for those who like more heat.

serves **6** • prep time **15 mins** • cooking time **4 hours on high/8 hours on low**

1 kg lamb shoulder, diced
4 tbsp olive oil
2 tsp ground cinnamon
1 tsp paprika
2 tsp crushed coriander seeds
2 tsp crushed cumin seeds
200 g green lentils
4 onions, sliced
2 carrots, diced

4 garlic cloves, chopped
2 x 400 g cans chickpeas, drained
  and rinsed
500 ml hot lamb stock
25 g coriander leaves and stalks
100 ml natural yoghurt
Salt and freshly ground black pepper
Flatbread, to serve

1 Season the lamb. Heat half the oil over a medium heat in a large frying pan and cook the lamb for about 10 minutes, until browned all over. Stir in the cinnamon, paprika, coriander and cumin and cook for a further 3 minutes, until the spices smell aromatic. Transfer to the slow cooker and stir in the lentils.

2 Heat the remaining oil over a medium heat in the pan and cook the onions, carrots and garlic for about 5 minutes, until softened. Transfer to the slow cooker and stir in the chickpeas.

3 Add the stock, season well and cook for 4 hours on the high setting or 8 hours on low.

4 About 15 minutes before the end of the cooking time, stir in the coriander and yoghurt. Serve with flatbread.

lancashire hotpot

Lamb middle neck chops are widely available at good butchers, although they are unlikely to be sold at supermarkets. They are essential for this dish, and are delicious in other braised lamb dishes too. Lambs' kidneys are cheap and also widely available. They add a richness to the sauce and break down during cooking.

serves **6** • prep time **20 mins** • cooking time **4 hours on high/8 hours on low**

1.4 kg lamb middle neck chops
Plain flour, for dusting
30 g butter
3 lambs' kidneys, chopped
800 g potatoes, sliced
3 onions, sliced

1 bay leaf
2 thyme sprigs
400 ml hot lamb stock
Salt and freshly ground black pepper
Steamed shredded greens, to serve

1 Season the lamb and dust with the flour. Heat the butter over a medium heat in a frying pan and cook the chops for about 5 minutes, until browned all over. Set the lamb aside and quickly fry the kidneys.

2 In the slow cooker, layer the lamb with the kidneys, potatoes and onions, seasoning each layer as you go, and finishing with a layer of potatoes. Tuck the bay leaf and thyme in between the layers.

3 Pour over the stock and cook for 4 hours on the high setting or 8 hours on low. Baste the potatoes with the juices once or twice.

4 Serve hot with the shredded steamed greens.

lamb with spring vegetables and aïoli

This light casserole, with its bulbous spring onions and new potatoes, heralds the first signs of spring. Cornish new potatoes are the first to come into season and have a delicious flavour all of their own.

serves **6** • prep time **20 mins** • cooking time **4 hours on high/8 hours on low**

1 kg lamb shoulder, diced
4 tbsp sunflower oil
12 large spring onions, trimmed
  and left whole
1 bay leaf
2 thyme sprigs
300 ml white wine
200 ml lamb stock
300 g Chantenay carrots, trimmed
200 g baby turnips, left whole
500 g baby new potatoes, cut to
  an even size

1 kg peas in the pod, shelled,
  or 300 g frozen garden peas
3 tbsp lemon thyme
2 garlic cloves
1 tsp coarse sea salt
2 tbsp mayonnaise
1 tbsp chopped flat-leaf parsley
Salt and freshly ground black pepper
2 tbsp crème fraîche, to serve

1 Season the lamb. Heat half the oil over a high heat in a frying pan and cook the lamb for about 10 minutes, until browned all over. Spoon into the slow cooker.

2 Heat the remaining oil over a medium heat in the pan and cook the spring onions for about 5 minutes, until softened. Season and then add the bay leaf, thyme, wine and stock and bring up to a simmer. Transfer to the slow cooker.

3 Stir in the carrots, turnips, potatoes, peas and lemon thyme and cook for 4 hours on the high setting or 8 hours on low.

4 To make the aïoli, chop the garlic, then crush it together the salt using the back of a knife. Stir this into the mayonnaise and add the parsley.

5 To serve, stir the crème fraîche into the lamb, and serve with the aïoli.

lamb tagine with couscous

serves **6** • prep time **15 mins** • cooking time **4 hours on high/8 hours on low**

800 g lean lamb shoulder, diced
3 tbsp olive oil
2 red onions, chopped
3 carrots, chopped
1 tbsp paprika
1 tbsp crushed coriander seeds
1 tbsp fennel seeds
3 cm piece cinnamon stick
4 garlic cloves, left whole
2 bay leaves

2 tbsp lime juice
500 ml chicken stock
150 g dried prunes
2 x 400 g cans chopped tomatoes
600 g couscous
Salt and freshly ground black pepper
4 tbsp chopped coriander, to serve
Harissa paste, to serve
Natural yoghurt, to serve

1 Season the lamb. Heat 2 tablespoons of the oil over a high heat in a large frying pan and cook the lamb, in batches if necessary, for about 10 minutes, until browned all over. Spoon into the slow cooker.

2 Heat the remaining oil over a medium heat in the pan and cook the onions and carrots for about 5 minutes, until softened. Add to the slow cooker.

3 In the same hot pan, heat the paprika, coriander seeds, fennel seeds and cinnamon for about 1 minute, until they start to smell aromatic. Also add to the slow cooker.

4 Stir in the garlic, bay leaves, lime juice, stock, prunes and chopped tomatoes, and season well. Cook for 4 hours on the high setting or 8 hours on low.

5 About 30 minutes before the end of the cooking time, spoon the couscous over the surface of the stew, cover and leave to steam until tender.

6 Serve the tagine and couscous garnished with the coriander and hand the yoghurt and harissa around separately.

greek-style lamb, potato and thyme kleftiko

Kleftiko is a Greek dish, its name meaning 'stolen lamb'. Bandits in the Greek hills would steal a lamb and cook it in a sealed pot set over an open fire. The sealing was important so that no smoke would escape and give away their position. The resulting kleftiko is a tremendously succulent dish.

serves **6** • prep time **15 mins** • cooking time **4 hours on high/8 hours on low**

1 kg shoulder of lamb, bone-in
3 tbsp chopped rosemary
2 onions, quartered
1 head garlic, cut in half horizontally
2 tomatoes, halved
4 waxy potatoes, quartered

250 ml chicken stock
100 ml olive oil
Sea salt and freshly ground
  black pepper
Pitta bread, to serve

1 With a sharp knife, make incisions all over the lamb and insert rosemary leaves into them. Rub all over with sea salt and freshly ground black pepper.

2 Put the onions, garlic, tomatoes and potatoes into the bottom of the slow cooker and rest the lamb shoulder on top. Pour over the stock and olive oil and cook for 4 hours on the high setting or 8 hours on low.

3 Serve with pitta bread to sop up the sauces.

italian lamb stew with olives and capers

serves **6** • prep time **20 mins** • cooking time **4 hours on high/8 hours on low**

4 tbsp olive oil
1 kg lamb shoulder, diced
300 ml white wine
1 onion, chopped
1 carrot, chopped
1 celery stick, chopped
4 garlic cloves, chopped
1 x 400 g can chopped tomatoes
200 ml lamb stock
Pared rind of 1 lemon

1 bay leaf
2 tbsp chopped thyme
300 g instant polenta, to serve
Salt and freshly ground black pepper
2 tbsp extra virgin olive oil
100 g black olives, chopped
4 tbsp salted capers, rinsed and
    chopped
Green beans, to serve

1 Heat half the oil over a medium heat in a large frying pan and cook the lamb for about 10 minutes, until browned all over. Season well and transfer to the slow cooker. Deglaze the pan with the white wine, scraping off any residues.

2 Heat the remaining oil over a medium heat and cook the onion, carrot, celery and garlic for about 5 minutes, until softened. Transfer to the slow cooker.

3 Add the tomatoes, stock, lemon rind, bay leaf and thyme to the slow cooker and add seasoning. Cook for 4 hours on the high setting or 8 hours on low.

4 To make the soft polenta, bring 1.5 litres of water to the boil and add salt. Add the polenta in a thin stream to avoid the water coming off the boil. Stir constantly for 5 minutes. Season with black pepper and the extra virgin olive oil.

5 Just before serving, stir the olives and capers into the stew. Spoon the lamb over the soft polenta and serve with the green beans.

massaman curry with lamb

Massaman, musoman or mastoman is an aromatic, very mild curry from Thailand. It's fine to use a good quality commercial paste, especially as it will be well cooked in the slow cooker. If you prefer, you can make your own paste and freeze it in small blocks for use in other recipes: simply blend 1 teaspoon each of coriander seeds, cumin seeds, ground cinnamon, cloves and white peppercorns with 1 whole star anise, 3 cardamom pods, 5 shallots, 6 garlic cloves, 1 lemongrass stalk, 2 tbsp chilli flakes (or to taste) and the grated zest of 1 lime. Season and use as directed.

serves **6** • prep time **20 mins** • cooking time **4 hours on high/8 hours on low**

2 tbsp sunflower oil
1.4 kg lamb, diced
2 onions, chopped
2 tbsp Thai massaman curry paste
300 ml lamb stock
200 ml coconut cream

350 g potatoes, roughly diced
75 g naturally roasted peanuts, shelled
Basmati rice, to serve
4 tbsp chopped coriander, to garnish

1 Heat the oil over a high heat in a saucepan and cook the lamb for about 10 minutes, until browned all over. Stir in the onions and curry paste and cook for about 5 minutes, until it smells aromatic. Add the stock.

2 Heat until nearly simmering, then transfer to the slow cooker. Add the coconut cream. Cook for 4 hours on the high setting or 8 hours on low.

3 About 20 minutes before the end of the cooking time, add the potatoes and the peanuts. Serve over rice, garnished with the fresh coriander.

braised lamb with rosemary and haricot beans and pesto dumplings

If you thought convenience food was a modern invention, think again. The addition of dumplings to a long-cooked stew means that no extra potatoes are needed – you've got a complete meal in one pot. These dumplings are flavoured with pesto to give an extra zing to the lamb.

serves **6** • prep time **15 mins** • cooking time **4 hours on high/8 hours on low**

1 kg diced lamb
3 tbsp olive oil
2 tbsp plain flour
2 onions, roughly chopped
2 carrots, roughly diced
3 garlic cloves, chopped
1 bay leaf
3 tbsp chopped rosemary

3 tbsp tomato purée
400 ml hot lamb stock
2 x 400 g cans haricot beans, drained
  and rinsed
2 tbsp basil pesto
100 g vegetable suet
100 g self-raising flour
Salt and freshly ground black pepper

1 Heat half the oil in a large frying pan over a high heat and cook the lamb for about 10 minutes, until browned all over. Transfer to the slow cooker and then stir in the plain flour.

2 Heat the remaining oil over a medium heat in the pan and cook the onions, carrots and garlic. Transfer to the slow cooker, season well and add the bay leaf, rosemary, tomato purée and stock. Stir in the beans. Cook for 4 hours on the high setting or 8 hours on low.

3 Start making the dumplings about 20 minutes before the end of the cooking time. Mix together the pesto, suet and self-raising flour in a bowl and season with salt. Stir 200 ml of water into the suet mix until a dough forms. Drop teaspoons of the dough on top of the casserole, cover and cook for 15 minutes.

4 Serve the lamb and dumplings immediately in warmed deep plates.

coconut and coriander lamb curry

This lamb curry will be a hit with all the family; it is mild but it has a variety of flavours that will suit even the most discerning palate. If you prefer a hotter curry, add a little chopped fresh chilli – enough to add some heat but not overpower it.

serves **6** • prep time **20 mins** • cooking time **4 hours on high/8 hours on low**

2 tbsp oil
1.2 kg lamb shoulder, diced
3 onions, chopped
4 garlic cloves, chopped
1 tbsp grated fresh root ginger
1 tbsp coriander seeds, crushed
4 cardamom pods, crushed

1 tbsp ground turmeric
1 tbsp chilli flakes
150 g coconut cream
300 ml hot lamb stock
400 g low-fat natural yoghurt
4 tbsp chopped coriander
350 g basmati rice, to serve

1 Heat half the oil in a large frying pan over a high heat and brown the lamb well all over. Transfer to the slow cooker.

2 Heat the remaining oil in the frying pan over a medium heat and stir in the onions, garlic, ginger, coriander seeds, cardamom, turmeric and chilli flakes until aromatic. Add to the slow cooker with the coconut cream, stock and yoghurt and cook for 4 hours on the high setting or 8 hours on low.

3 About 20 minutes before the end of the cooking time, add the coriander and cook the basmati rice according to the packet instructions.

4 Serve hot over the rice.

lamb pilaf with tzatziki and coriander

I love to serve tzatziki or houmous, if you prefer, with pilaf; they add a fresh flavour, and a creamy dimension to the texture of the dish.

serves **6** • prep time **15 mins** • cooking time **3 hours on high/6 hours on low**

6 tbsp olive oil
1 large mild onion, chopped
2 carrots, chopped
1 bay leaf
1 tbsp coriander seeds, crushed
1 tbsp cumin seeds
3 garlic cloves, chopped
500 g lamb shoulder, diced

250 g brown rice, washed
800 ml lamb stock
50 g coriander, chopped
4 tomatoes, chopped
6 spring onions, finely sliced
150 g tzatziki
6 lemon wedges

1 Heat half the oil in a large frying pan over a medium heat. Add the onion, carrots, bay leaf, coriander seeds, cumin seeds and garlic and fry for 3–4 minutes until the spices are aromatic and the onion is softened. Transfer to the slow cooker.

2 Heat the remaining oil in the frying pan and brown the lamb all over. Stir in the rice and coat it in the oil. Transfer to the slow cooker.

3 Pour over the stock and cook for 3 hours on the high setting or 6 hours on low.

4 At the end of the cooking time, mix together the coriander, tomatoes and spring onions in a bowl to make a salsa. Serve the pilaf with the salsa and tzatziki on the side, with some lemon wedges.

lamb with apricots and couscous

Couscous makes a fantastic speedy midweek meal and it perfectly offsets this lamb dish, which is packed with goodness. Lamb, apricot and spices are a classic North African combination, and the aroma of this cooking will make you feel as if you're in warmer climes!

serves **6** • prep time **15 mins** • cooking time **4 hours on high/8 hours on low**

800 g lean diced lamb
3 tbsp olive oil
2 mild onions, chopped
2 carrots, chopped
1 waxy potato, peeled and diced
1 tbsp paprika
3 cm piece cinnamon stick
1 tbsp fennel seeds
4 garlic cloves, left whole

1 bay leaf
500 ml hot chicken stock
400 g couscous
150 g dried apricots, soaked and halved, or ready-to-eat apricots, halved
4 tbsp chopped coriander, to serve
Natural yoghurt, to serve
Salt and freshly ground black pepper

1 Season the lamb. Heat 2 tablespoons of the oil in a large frying pan over a high heat. Brown the lamb, in batches if necessary, and spoon into the slow cooker.

2 Heat the remaining oil in the frying pan and brown the onions, carrots and potato. Stir in the paprika, cinnamon and fennel seeds, then transfer everything to the slow cooker. Season well.

3 Add the garlic, bay leaf and stock and cook for 4 hours on the high setting or 8 hours on low.

4 About 30 minutes before the end of the cooking time, pour boiling water over the couscous and leave to stand for 10 minutes. Mix together the couscous and apricots and spoon it over the surface of the tagine. Replace the lid and let the couscous steam until tender.

5 Serve with the couscous sprinkled with coriander, and the yoghurt handed round separately.

lamb and cauliflower kashmir curry

Middle-neck lamb chops are perfect for slow cooking as they need to be cooked out for a length of time to tenderise and for their full flavour to be released. The bone means that the chops hold together well during cooking and also remain succulent.

serves **6–8** • prep time **15 mins** • cooking time **4 hours on high/8 hours on low**

1 kg middle-neck lamb chops
4 tbsp oil
3 onions, sliced
4 garlic cloves, chopped
250 g cauliflower in florets
50 g Kashmiri curry paste
1 tbsp ground turmeric

100 g whole almonds
200 ml hot lamb stock
300 ml natural low-fat yoghurt
2 tsp cornflour
350 g basmati rice, 1 cardamom pod and
  1 bay leaf, to serve
Salt and freshly ground black pepper

1 Season the meat. Heat half the oil in a large frying pan over a high heat and brown the chops on both sides. Add them to the slow cooker.

2 Heat the remaining oil in the frying pan and cook the onions and garlic for about 5 minutes over a medium heat until well softened. Add the cauliflower for the last 2 minutes then transfer everything to the slow cooker.

3 Stir in the curry paste, turmeric, almonds and stock. In a bowl, mix together the yoghurt and cornflour and add this to the slow cooker. Cook for 4 hours on the high setting or 8 hours on low.

4 Just before serving, cook the basmati rice according to the packet instructions, adding the cardamom pod and bay leaf to the pan. Serve the hot curry over the flavoured basmati rice.

lamb and chickpea moroccan stew

Stews like this one are perfect in the slow cooker – economical, tasty and requiring minimum preparation. It's the perfect restorative supper dish after a long day at work or school.

serves: **6** • prep time **15 mins** • cooking time **4 hours on high/8 hours on low**

800 g lean diced lamb
3 tbsp olive oil
2 onions, chopped
3 carrots, chopped
3 celery sticks, chopped
1 tbsp coriander seeds, crushed
1 tbsp cumin seeds
1 tbsp ground cinnamon
4 garlic cloves, left whole

400 g can chickpeas, drained
500 ml hot chicken stock
400 g can chopped tomatoes, or 450 g
   fresh tomatoes, roughly chopped
600 g couscous
Salt and freshly ground black pepper
Lemon wedges, harissa paste and
   natural yoghurt

1 Season the lamb. Heat 2 tablespoons of the oil in a large frying pan over a high heat. Brown the lamb, in batches if necessary, and spoon into the slow cooker.

2 Heat the remaining oil in the frying pan and brown the onions, carrots and celery over a medium heat for 5 minutes. Add the coriander seeds, cumin seeds, cinnamon and garlic and transfer everything to the slow cooker.

3 Stir in the chickpeas, stock and tomatoes and season well. Cook for 4 hours on the high setting or 8 hours on low.

4 About 30 minutes before the end of the cooking time, pour boiling water over the couscous and leave to stand for 10 minutes. Spoon the soaked couscous over the surface of the stew, replace the lid and let the couscous steam for the remaining cooking time.

5 Serve the stew with the couscous, and with the lemon wedges, harissa and yoghurt handed round separately.

hearty pork casserole with apples

A classic combination that evokes the aromas and flavours of autumn. The sharpness of the apples cuts through the pork beautifully.

serves **6** • prep time **20 mins** • cooking time **4 hours on high/8 hours on low**

1.2 kg pork shoulder, diced
2 tbsp olive oil
2 leeks, roughly chopped
1 turnip, roughly chopped
1 celery stick, roughly chopped
2 Granny Smith apples, cored and chopped
200 g streaky bacon, each rasher cut into 3
3 tbsp dried mixed herbs

1 bay leaf
100 ml cider
300 ml hot chicken stock
1 tbsp black treacle
2 tsp mustard powder
$\frac{1}{2}$ Savoy cabbage, shredded
2.5 kg Maris Piper potatoes, chopped
50 g butter
100 ml milk
Salt and freshly ground black pepper

1   Season the pork. Heat half the oil in a large frying pan over a high heat and brown the pork, in batches if necessary. Transfer to the slow cooker.

2   Heat the remaining oil and cook the leeks, turnip, celery, apples and bacon over a high heat, stirring for approximately 5 minutes, until golden. Spoon into the slow cooker and stir in the mixed herbs with the bay leaf.

3   Add the cider, stock, black treacle and mustard powder, mix well, season, and cook for 4 hours on the high setting or 8 hours on low.

4   To make the mashed potato, 30 minutes before serving put the potatoes in a pan with enough cold salted water to cover. Bring to the boil then cook, uncovered, for 15 minutes or until tender, then drain. Return the potatoes to the pan with the butter and milk and season well. Mash with a potato masher for some texture, or use a potato ricer or food mill if you prefer a smoother version.

5   About 15 minutes before the end of the cooking time, stir the cabbage into the casserole. Serve piping hot with the mashed potato.

pork casserole with mustard dumplings

serves **6** • prep time **20 mins** • cooking time **4 hours on high/8 hours on low**

1 kg pork shoulder, diced
2 tbsp sunflower oil
1 leek, trimmed and roughly chopped
1 onion, roughly chopped
1 turnip, roughly chopped
1 carrot, roughly chopped
1 celery stick, roughly chopped
200 g streaky bacon, each rasher cut
  into three
3 tbsp mixed chopped herbs

1 bay leaf
200 g dried prunes, stoned
100 ml beer
300 ml pork stock
125 g vegetable suet
100 g self-raising flour
2 tsp mustard powder
½ Savoy cabbage, shredded
Salt and freshly ground black pepper

1 Season the pork. Heat half the oil in a large saucepan over a high heat and cook the pork until browned all over. Spoon into the slow cooker.

2 Heat the remaining oil on a medium heat in the saucepan and cook the leek, onion, turnip, carrot, celery and bacon for about 10 minutes, until softened. Stir in the mixed herbs and bay leaf, then spoon the mixture into the slow cooker.

3 Add the prunes, beer and stock, mix well and season. Cook for 4 hours on the high setting or 8 hours on low.

4 Start making the dumplings about 30 minutes before the end of the cooking time. Mix together the suet, flour and mustard in a bowl, add seasoning and set aside.

5 About 20 minutes before the end of the cooking time, stir the cabbage into the casserole. Stir 200 ml water into the suet mix until it forms a dough. Place teaspoonfuls of the dough on top of the casserole, cover and cook for 15 minutes. If you plan to hold the casserole in the slow cooker, cook the cabbage and the dumplings separately to serve. Steam them over boiling water, or cook in boiling vegetable stock to cover, for 15 minutes.

6 Top each portion with a mustard dumpling and a good amount of sauce and serve with the cabbage.

thai pork curry with lime leaf and coconut

This dish is ideal for the frugal slow cook. Tender cuts of pork have been replaced by the inexpensive shoulder, which will tenderise over long cooking and produce a much tastier result than more expensive pork fillet. The curry also freezes well: in this case, make it without the lime juice, fish sauce and herbs and add them when reheating it.

serves **6** • prep time **20 mins** • cooking time **4 hours on high/8 hours on low**

1 tbsp sunflower oil	8 dried lime leaves
1 kg pork shoulder, diced	1 red pepper, deseeded and chopped
1 onion, sliced	6 baby aubergines, quartered
90 g red Thai curry paste	2 tbsp chopped coriander leaves
6 tbsp lime juice	2 tbsp chopped basil leaves
1 x 440 ml can coconut milk	4 tbsp fish sauce
2 tbsp soy sauce	Thai jasmine rice, to serve

1 Heat the oil in a saucepan over a high heat and cook the pork and onion for about 5 minutes, until browned all over. Transfer to the slow cooker.

2 Combine the curry paste with half the lime juice and all the coconut milk, soy sauce and lime leaves. Heat to a simmer and pour over the pork. Add the red pepper. Cook for 4 hours on the high setting, or 8 hours on low.

3 About 15 minutes before the end of the cooking time, stir in the aubergines together with the remaining lime juice and the coriander, basil and fish sauce.

4 To serve, spoon portions of the curry over cooked jasmine rice in large bowls.

szechuan braised belly of pork

Belly pork has a naturally juicy texture and a flavour that marries well with oriental ingredients. The high fat content keeps the pork from drying out over a long cooking time, allowing the spices to infuse the meat. This dish has a lot of broth, so I suggest eating some with the pork and serving the rest over a bowl of noodles.

serves **6** • prep time **15 mins** • cooking time **4 hours on high/8 hours on low**

1 kg boneless belly pork, rind removed
   and cut into 5 cm cubes
60 g piece fresh root ginger, grated
2 garlic cloves, chopped
3 star anise
1 cinnamon stick
2 tsp mustard powder

1 tsp chilli flakes
100 ml light soy sauce
400 ml chicken stock
100 ml rice wine
6 spring onions, halved
3 heads pak choi, quartered
375 g medium egg noodles, to serve

1 Place the pork in a large saucepan, cover with boiling water, return to the boil and then leave to simmer for 5 minutes. Drain well and transfer the pork to the slow cooker.

2 Put the ginger, garlic, star anise, cinnamon, mustard powder, chilli flakes, soy sauce, stock and rice wine in the saucepan, bring to the boil and then let simmer for 2 minutes. Add to the slow cooker together with the spring onions and cook for 4 hours on the high setting or 8 hours on low.

3 About 5 minutes before the end of the cooking time, add the pak choi leaves to the slow cooker. Stir through and cook for a further 5 minutes, until wilted.

4 Serve some of the broth and the pak choi over the diced pork belly on plates, and pour the remaining broth over individual bowls of noodles.

satay-style pork with coriander

The flavours of satay are easy to love: pleasantly sweet and creamy, but not too hot. The combination of peanuts, coconut and pork make this quite a rich dish, so serve it with lots of rice to balance it out.

serves **6** • prep time **20 mins** • cooking time **4 hours on high/8 hours on low**

2 tbsp sunflower oil
650 g pork shoulder, diced
2 onions, chopped
1 green pepper, deseeded and sliced
2 carrots, sliced
3 garlic cloves, chopped
1 tbsp lemon juice
1 tbsp tahini paste
4 tbsp peanut butter

2 tbsp chilli flakes (or to taste)
2 tbsp dark soy sauce
200 ml coconut cream
200 g frozen soy beans
Cellophane rice noodles, to serve
Coriander leaves, to garnish
Red pepper slices, to garnish
Lemon wedges, to serve

1 Heat the oil over a high heat in a large saucepan. Cook the pork for about 5 minutes, until browned all over then stir in the onions, green pepper and carrots and cook for a further 5 minutes, until softened.

2 Stir in the garlic, lemon juice, tahini paste, peanut butter, chilli flakes, soy sauce and coconut cream. Transfer to the slow cooker and cook for 4 hours on the high setting or 8 hours on low.

3 About 15 minutes before the end of the cooking time, add the soy beans.

4 Serve the pork over noodles, garnished with the coriander leaves and red pepper and with the lemon wedges alongside.

sausage, red onion and bean casserole

This is great for a midweek family supper. If your family aren't keen on spicy food, simply replace the merguez sausages with ordinary pork or beef ones. Chipotle chillies are Mexican, with a fiery heat to them. Chipotle paste (available from supermarkets) is a really convenient and accurate way of adding them because fresh chillies can be random in their heat levels. There's also no need to scrub your hands and the chopping board as you would after preparing a fresh chilli.

serves **6** • prep time **20 mins** • cooking time **4 hours on high/8 hours on low**

2 tbsp sunflower oil
2 red onions, diced
1 carrot, diced
450 g merguez sausages
450 g pork sausages
2 garlic cloves, chopped
½ tsp chipotle chilli paste
200 ml beef stock

2 x 400 g cans chopped tomatoes
1 tbsp chopped rosemary
100 g pinto beans, soaked overnight,
    or 1 x 420 g can of pinto beans,
    drained and rinsed
Salt and freshly ground black pepper
Jacket potatoes, to serve
Sour cream, to serve

1 Heat half the oil over a medium heat in a frying pan and add the onions and carrot. Cook for 5 minutes and then transfer to the slow cooker.

2 Heat the remaining oil over a medium heat in the frying pan and cook the sausages for about 10 minutes, until browned all over. Add the garlic, chilli paste, stock and tomatoes. Bring to a simmer and then add to the slow cooker.

3 Season well and then stir in the chopped rosemary and pinto beans. Cook for 4 hours on the high setting or 8 hours on low.

4 Serve with jacket potatoes and sour cream.

beef with beetroot, parsnips and horseradish cream

In this recipe a usually tough cut of meat becomes meltingly tender through gentle slow cooking, and its flavour is enhanced by the sweetness of the beetroot and parsnips. The horseradish cream is an ideal accompaniment if you want to add a bit of a kick to the dish.

serves **6** • prep time **15 mins** • cooking time **4 hours on high/8 hours on low**

1.4 kg beef stewing steak, diced
2 tbsp oil
30 g butter
2 tbsp plain flour
2 onions, cut into wedges
350 g beetroot, peeled and
  cut into wedges
350 g parsnips, peeled and
  cut into wedges

1 bay leaf
1 large sprig of thyme
3 tbsp chopped mixed herbs
300 ml hot beef stock
3 tbsp creamed horseradish, to serve
3 tbsp soured cream, to serve
Salt and freshly ground black pepper

1 Season the beef. Heat half the oil and the butter in a large frying pan over a high heat. Cook the beef in batches until well browned. Spoon into the slow cooker and stir in the flour.

2 Heat the remaining butter and oil in the frying pan and brown the onions, beetroot and parsnips. Transfer everything to the slow cooker, add the bay leaf, thyme, mixed herbs and stock and cook for 4 hours on the high setting or 8 hours on low.

3 Meanwhile, mix together the horseradish and soured cream in a small bowl and season well.

4 Serve the beef hot with the horseradish cream and, if you like, some green vegetables of your choice.

rich beef casserole

This is a classic yet simple beef casserole with a silky, hearty sauce that coats the meat and vegetables beautifully, just inviting some warm crusty bread to mop up the juices. If you want to pep up your 5-a-day, serve it with some steamed seasonal green vegetables.

serves **4** • prep time **20 mins** • cooking time **4 hours on high/8 hours on low**

2 tbsp sunflower or olive oil
50 g butter
750 g beef stewing steak, diced
1 tsp cayenne pepper
300 ml hot beef stock
150 g streaky bacon, each rasher
   cut into 3
250 g carrots, peeled and cut into
   large chunks

2 onions, peeled and roughly chopped
1 celery stick, chopped
30 g plain flour
2 bay leaves
2 tbsp thyme leaves
Salt and freshly ground black pepper

1   Heat half the oil and butter in a large frying pan over a high heat. Season the beef and stir in the cayenne pepper. Cook the beef in batches until well browned and spoon into the slow cooker. Pour a little of the stock into the frying pan to deglaze it and use a wooden spoon to scrape off any residue. Transfer to the slow cooker.

2   Heat the remaining oil and butter in the frying pan and brown the bacon, carrots, onions and celery. Transfer to the slow cooker.

3   Stir the flour into the casserole mixture, add the bay leaf, thyme and remaining stock and cook for 4 hours on the high setting or 8 hours on low.

4   Check the seasoning and serve the casserole piping hot.

spaghetti bolognese

This is a staple in my house, as it is in many households, regularly making an appearance on the table. It is based on a ragù (meat sauce) from Bologna, the capital city of Emilia-Romagna in northern Italy, where the cuisine is based on rich sauces. Traditionally, bolognese sauce is served over spaghetti, but it is also good spooned over hot jacket potatoes, or used on pizza with mozzarella.

serves **6** • prep time **15 mins** • cooking time **4 hours on high/8 hours on low**

1 kg minced beef
2 tbsp olive oil
2 onions, chopped
2 carrots, chopped
2 celery sticks, chopped
4 garlic cloves, chopped
100 ml red wine
2 tbsp tomato purée

1 x 400 g can chopped tomatoes
2 bay leaves
2 tbsp milk
1 tbsp dried oregano
Salt and freshly ground black pepper
Spaghetti, to serve
Grated Parmesan, to serve

1   Heat half the oil over a high heat in a large frying pan and cook the mince for about 5 minutes, until browned all over. Season well and transfer to the slow cooker.

2   Heat the remaining oil over a medium heat in the pan and cook the onions, carrots and celery for about 5 minutes, until softened. Stir in the garlic and spoon into the slow cooker.

3   Pour the red wine into the pan and heat to deglaze it, then add the tomato purée, chopped tomatoes, bay leaves, milk and oregano and add seasoning. When it reaches a simmer, transfer to the slow cooker. Cook for 4 hours on the high setting or 8 hours on low.

4   To serve, cook the spaghetti according to the packet instructions. Drain, divide between individual bowls and top with the sauce, handing around the grated Parmesan separately.

vietnamese beef with rice noodles

Fresh herbs, texture and red hot chilli with fish sauce sour notes are the hallmarks of Vietnamese cuisine. Although the ingredients are familiar from Chinese, Malaysian and Thai food, their use in Vietnamese cooking is fresher and lighter.

serves **6** • prep time **15 mins** • cooking time **4 hours on high/8 hours on low**

3 tbsp sunflower oil
800 g braising steak, cut into slices
   5 mm thick
2 onions, sliced
2 carrots, sliced
3 garlic cloves, crushed
400 ml chicken stock
4 dried lime leaves
1 lemongrass stalk, bruised
2 red chillies (or to taste), deseeded
   and chopped

Salt and freshly ground black pepper
Flat rice noodles, to serve
6 tbsp chopped roasted peanuts,
   to serve, to serve
Soy sauce, to serve
100 g beansprouts, to serve
1 cucumber, finely chopped, to serve
Large handful mint leaves, to serve
Large handful coriander leaves, to serve

1 Heat half the oil in a large frying pan over a high heat and cook the beef for about 3 minutes, until browned all over. Season and transfer to the slow cooker.

2 Heat the remaining oil in the pan over a high heat and stir-fry the onions, carrots and garlic. Season and transfer to the slow cooker.

3 Add the stock to the slow cooker together with the lime leaves and lemongrass. The chillies can be added now or handed around separately as a garnish when serving, for diners to add to their own taste. Season well. Cook for 4 hours on the high setting or 8 hours on low.

4 Serve over rice noodles, sprinkled with the chopped peanuts. Hand around the soy sauce, beansprouts, cucumber, mint leaves and coriander leaves separately for people to add as desired.

chinese beef with green peppers and black bean sauce

The pronounced flavour of the green peppers mellows out over time when cooked with the black beans and beef. Serve this dish over noodles for a Friday night alternative to takeaway.

serves **6** • prep time **15 mins** • cooking time **4 hours on high/8 hours on low**

4 tbsp groundnut oil
2 green peppers, deseeded and roughly
  diced
2 onions, cut into wedges
4 garlic cloves, crushed
10 cm piece fresh root ginger, grated
700 g chuck steak, cut into 5 mm slices
3 tbsp cornflour

200 ml chicken stock
100 ml rice wine
100 ml soy sauce
150 ml oyster sauce
1 x 400 g can black beans, drained
  and rinsed
6 spring onions, thinly sliced, to garnish
Egg noodles, to serve

1 Heat half the oil over a high heat in a large frying pan or wok. Add the peppers, onions, garlic and ginger and stir-fry for about 30 seconds until hot. Transfer to the slow cooker.

2 Toss the beef in the cornflour. Heat the remaining oil over a high heat in the pan or wok and stir-fry the beef for about 3 minutes, until browned all over.

3 Add the chicken stock, heat through and transfer the mixture to the slow cooker. Stir in the rice wine, soy and and oyster sauces and the black beans. Cook for 4 hours on the high setting or 8 hours on low.

4 Serve over noodles in large bowls garnished with the spring onions.

game casserole with winter vegetables

Game is fast becoming popular as an alternative to the more traditional chicken. It is widely available in supermarkets, generally between August and February when it comes into season, and is the ultimate organic meat.

serves **6** • prep time **15 mins** • cooking time **4 hours on high/8 hours on low**

800 g mixed game pack, diced
4 tbsp butter
1 tbsp plain flour
2 onions, chopped
2 carrots, diced
½ a celeriac, peeled and diced
3 small turnips, peeled and quartered
300 ml hot game stock

1 bay leaf
2 tbsp thyme, chopped
1 parsnip, peeled and thinly sliced
3 tbsp olive oil
3 tbsp chopped flat-leaf parsley,
   to serve
Salt and freshly ground black pepper

1 Season the game. Heat half the butter in a large frying pan over a medium heat and seal the game. Transfer to the slow cooker and stir in the flour.

2 Heat the remaining butter and soften the onions, carrots, celeriac and turnips over a medium heat. Transfer to the slow cooker. Add the stock, bay leaf and thyme and cook for 4 hours on the high setting or 8 hours on low.

3 Meanwhile, fry the parsnip slices in a frying pan with the oil over a medium heat, until just golden.

4 Serve piping hot with the fried parsnip and scattered with the parsley.

curried rabbit casserole

Rabbit's firm, meaty flesh is excellent for casseroles and stews, and its strong flavour works particularly well in a curry. This is not too spicy for children and those with sensitive palates, but if you prefer more heat, increase the cayenne content to taste.

serves **4** • prep time **15 mins** • cooking time **4 hours on high/8 hours on low**

1 kg rabbit pieces, or	1 tsp cayenne pepper (optional)
1 whole rabbit, jointed	1 bay leaf
4 tbsp oil	200 ml hot chicken stock
4 garlic cloves, crushed	250 g basmati rice, to serve
2 onions, chopped	4 tbsp crème fraîche
2 carrots, diced	Mango chutney, to serve
2 tbsp medium curry powder	Salt and freshly ground black pepper

1 Season the rabbit. Heat half the oil in a large frying pan over a high heat and brown the meat well. Transfer to the slow cooker.

2 Heat the remaining oil and soften the garlic, onions and carrots over a medium heat. Stir in the curry powder, cayenne (if using) and the bay leaf. Transfer everything to the slow cooker.

3 Deglaze the pan with a little of the stock and add to the slow cooker with the rest of the stock. Season well then cook for 4 hours on the high setting or 8 hours on low.

4 Just before serving, cook the rice according to the packet instructions and stir the crème fraîche into the rabbit casserole. Serve with the rice and a dollop of mango chutney.

VEGETARIAN AND VEGETABLE DISHES

hearty ribollita

Like numerous Italian dishes, ribollita has so many variations that no two bowls of this soup-cum-stew are ever the same. I'd like to say that this is an authentic version, but, to err on the side of caution, I'll say it's inspired by the Tuscan dish. Keep this dish true to its peasant roots by using up whatever vegetables you have spare.

serves **4-6** • prep time **20 mins** • cooking time **4 hours on high/8 hours on low**

3 tbsp olive oil
2 onions, peeled and diced
2 carrots, diced
3 celery sticks, diced
6 garlic cloves, thinly sliced
3 tbsp freshly chopped rosemary
2 tsp fennel seeds, lightly crushed
Large pinch of chilli flakes
2 bay leaves
400 g can cannellini beans, drained
    and rinsed
400 g can plum tomatoes,
    roughly crushed

1 litre hot vegetable stock
125 g stale good-quality bread, such as
    ciabatta or sourdough, torn into
    small chunks
250 g cavolo nero or chard thickly sliced
    (if using cavolo nero, blanch in boiling
    water for 2 minutes before adding to
    the pot)
Best-quality extra virgin olive oil,
    to serve
Salt and freshly ground black pepper

1   Heat the oil in a large frying pan over a medium heat, add the onions, carrots, celery, garlic, rosemary, fennel seeds, chilli flakes and bay leaves and cook for 5 minutes until starting to soften. Transfer to the slow cooker, add the beans, tomatoes, stock, bread and season well. Cook for 4 hours on the high setting or 8 hours on low.

2   About 20 minutes before the end of the cooking time, add the cavolo nero or chard and continue cooking.

3   Serve in large bowls, with a good glug of extra virgin olive oil drizzled over.

layered potato, pancetta and gruyère bake

This is a rich, rustic dish, perfect for a winter's evening. You can serve it by itself, but for that extra comfort factor, you might like to try it with sausages – that will really guarantee you keep out the cold! If you'd like to make it vegetarian you can simply leave out the pancetta.

serves **6** • prep time **15 mins** • cooking time **4 hours on high/8 hours on low**

1.2 kg potatoes, sliced
2 onions, sliced
140 g grated Gruyère cheese
140 g pancetta, chopped and fried
2 garlic cloves, left whole

100 ml double cream
4 tbsp fresh breadcrumbs
50 g butter
Salt and freshly ground black pepper

1 Layer the potatoes, onions, cheese and pancetta in the slow cooker, tucking in the garlic between layers. Season each layer and then pour the cream over the top.

2 Sprinkle the surface with the breadcrumbs and dabs of butter. Cook for 4 hours on the high setting or 8 hours on low.

3 Serve the bake either hot or cold.

white bean and tomato cassoulet
with walnut pesto

A perky dollop of zingy, fresh pesto adds a bit of zest to this hearty but healthy long-cooked cassoulet.

serves **6** • prep time **20 mins** • cooking time **4 hours on high/8 hours on low**

175 ml olive oil
1 mild onion, chopped
5 garlic cloves, left whole
2 carrots, chopped
2 celery sticks, chopped
2 x 400 g cans chopped tomatoes, drained
1 x 680 g bottle tomato passata
2 tbsp sage
2 tbsp thyme

2 x 400 g cans haricot beans, drained and rinsed
2 x 400 g cans butter beans, drained and rinsed
Pinch of sugar
50 g walnuts, roasted
50 g flat-leaf parsley
100 ml olive oil
50 g Pecorino cheese, grated
Salt and freshly ground black pepper

1   Heat 2 tablespoons of the oil over a medium heat in a saucepan and cook the onion, 3 of the garlic cloves, the carrots and celery for about 5 minutes, until softened. Spoon into the slow cooker.

2   In the same pan, heat the tomatoes and passata and season well. Pour into the slow cooker with the sage, thyme, haricot beans, butter beans, sugar and 3 tablespoons of the oil. Cook for 4 hours on the high setting or 8 hours on low.

3   To make the pesto, put the walnuts, the remaining 2 garlic cloves, parsley and Pecorino cheese in a food processor. Add the remaining 100 ml olive oil and season with freshly ground black pepper (no salt, because there's already lots in the Pecorino). Whiz together until a paste forms.

4   Serve the bean cassoulet with the pesto spooned over to taste.

ratatouille with potato wedges

serves **6** • prep time **15 mins** • cooking time **4 hours on high/8 hours on low**

3 red onions, cut into wedges
1 red pepper, deseeded and cut into 3 cm chunks
1 green pepper, deseeded and cut into 3 cm chunks
1 yellow pepper, deseeded and cut into 3 cm chunks
7 tbsp olive oil
Pinch of chilli flakes (optional)
2 x 400 g cans tomatoes, drained and chopped in the can
1 tsp sugar
4 garlic cloves, sliced
2 tsp dried oregano or marjoram
20 g basil leaves, roughly chopped
4 tbsp sun-dried tomato paste
4 courgettes, cut into chunks
700 g pumpkin, unpeeled (see page 109) and cut into 3 cm chunks
2 aubergines, cut into 3 cm chunks
Salt and freshly ground black pepper
2 kg waxy potatoes, cut into wedges
1 tbsp mild chilli powder

1 Preheat the oven to 220°C/Gas 7. Place the onions and peppers in a large baking tin. Drizzle with 5 tablespoons of the oil, and season with salt, freshly ground pepper and chilli flakes, if using. Mix to coat and roast for 20–25 minutes, until golden. Transfer to the slow cooker.

2 Meanwhile, heat the tomatoes with the sugar, garlic, 2 teaspoons of the oregano, half the basil and the tomato paste until simmering, and then pour into the slow cooker.

3 Add the courgettes, pumpkin and aubergines, stir and cook for 4 hours on the high setting or 8 hours on low.

4 Start making the potato wedges, about 30 minutes before the end of the cooking time. Preheat the oven to 180°C/Gas 4. In a baking tin, toss the potato wedges with the remaining 2 tablespoons of oil, the chilli powder and the remaining 2 teaspoons of oregano and bake in the oven for 20 minutes.

5 Stir the remaining basil through the ratatouille before serving with the potato wedges.

blackeye bean and chipotle chilli

The blackeye bean, also known as 'blackeyed peas' and 'cow beans', is a popular ingredient in Mexican food, which inspired this recipe. The beans marry nicely with the warmth from the chilli, and are widely used in spicy Creole cuisine. The heat from the chilli is offset by eating the stew with guacamole.

serves **6** • prep time **15 mins** • cooking time **4 hours on high/8 hours on low**

3 tbsp sunflower oil
1 large mild onion, chopped
2 carrots, chopped
2 garlic cloves, chopped
1 red pepper, deseeded and chopped
1 green pepper, deseeded and chopped
3 x 420 g cans black beans, drained
   and rinsed
1 tbsp tomato purée

500 ml chicken stock
2 whole dried chipotle chillies
Salt and freshly ground black pepper
2 ripe avocados, chopped
2 limes
2 tomatoes, chopped
3 tbsp sour cream
Tabasco, to taste
12 taco shells, to serve

1 Heat the oil over a medium heat in a saucepan and cook the onion, carrots, garlic, and peppers for 4–5 minutes, until softened. Add to the slow cooker.

2 Stir in the black beans, tomato purée, stock and seasoning. Cut the stalks from the chillies and add them to the pot. Cook for 4 hours on the high setting or 8 hours on low.

3 Start making the guacamole about 10 minutes before the end of the cooking time. Put the avocado flesh in a bowl and squeeze over the limes. Stir in the tomatoes, sour cream and Tabasco and adjust the seasoning.

4 To serve, warm the taco shells and invite people to spoon the beans into them then top them with the guacamole.

VEGETARIAN AND VEGETABLE DISHES

pine nut, fennel and parmesan risotto

There are three kinds of risotto rice that are widely available – Arborio, Carnaroli and Vialone Nano. If I am cooking a risotto on the hob, I use Arborio, which gives a pleasant texture because it breaks down after absorbing a certain amount of liquid. For the rice to absorb the flavours of the dish and hold texture over a few hours, it is worth seeking out Vialone Nano; it will give a creamy sauce and the rice will still have 'bite'. It is widely available from delicatessens and some supermarkets. Arborio will do as a substitute. You can also experiment with different flavours in the risotto by adding other vegetables at the end: try stirring in some steamed asparagus, fresh peas or stir-fried courgette along with the rocket.

serves **6** • prep time **15 mins** • cooking time **4 hours on low**

3 tbsp olive oil
2 onions, chopped
4 fennel heads, trimmed and sliced
   thinly
3 garlic cloves, chopped
500 g vialone nano risotto rice
2 bay leaves

250 ml white wine
2 litres vegetable stock
125 g pinenuts, roasted
100 g Parmesan, grated
25 g dill, chopped
100 g wild rocket
Salt and freshly ground black pepper

1 Heat the oil in a large saucepan over a medium heat and cook the onions, fennel and garlic for about 10 minutes, until softened, but not coloured.

2 Add the rice, bay leaves and wine and cook for a few minutes, until the mixture is heated through.

3 Add the stock and bring to the boil before transferring to the slow cooker. Stir in the pine nuts. Cover and cook for 4 hours on the low setting.

4 Stir through the Parmesan, dill and rocket before serving.

lebanese pilaf with wholegrains

Spelt is a very useful, healthy wholegrain, which is now widely available. It has a low gluten content, which is tolerated by a lot of people who cannot otherwise tolerate gluten. However, it is not suitable for coeliacs. Like the Lebanese dish tabbouleh, this one has fresh herbs added at the end for lots of colour and flavour. Try serving it as an accompaniment to a main course: it goes well with grilled fish, particularly salmon or mackerel. It is also delicious as an accompaniment to barbecued food.

serves **6** • prep time **15 mins** • cooking time **6 hours on low**

6 tbsp olive oil
1 large mild onion, chopped
1 bay leaf
2 tsp coriander seeds, crushed
2 tsp cumin seeds
1 tsp chilli flakes
3 garlic cloves, chopped
150 g brown rice, washed
150 g spelt grain, washed
150 g Puy lentils, washed

100 g ready-to-eat dried apricots, chopped
50 g pistachio nuts, toasted
1.8 litres vegetable stock
25 g mint, chopped
25 g coriander, chopped
25 g flat-leaf parsley, chopped
6 spring onions, finely sliced
Salt and freshly ground black pepper

1 Heat the oil over a medium heat in a saucepan. Add the onion, bay leaf, coriander and cumin seeds, chilli flakes and garlic and fry for 3–4 minutes, until the spices are smelling aromatic and the onion has softened.

2 Stir in the rice, spelt grain, lentils, apricots, pistachios and seasoning and mix to coat in the oil. Transfer to the slow cooker.

3 Pour in the stock and cook for 6 hours on the low setting.

4 Before serving, mix together the mint, coriander, parsley and spring onions and stir through the pilaf. Eat while hot.

bombay potato

There are as many varieties of Bombay potato as there are cooks in India, and not one of those cooks will give away their recipe. This is my own version, which I think is very close to the one I tried in Bombay.

serves **8** • prep time **20 mins** • cooking time **4 hours on high/8 hours on low**

4 tbsp butter
3 onions, sliced
4 garlic cloves, chopped
1 tbsp ground turmeric
½ tsp cumin seeds
½ tsp mustard seeds
½ tsp fennel seeds

1.6 kg waxy potatoes, quartered
   lengthways
3 tbsp tomato purée
1 x 400 g can chopped tomatoes
300 ml natural yoghurt
Salt
Basmati rice, to serve

1 Heat the butter in a large saucepan over a medium heat and cook the onions and garlic for about 5 minutes, until softened. Transfer to the slow cooker.

2 In the dry pan, heat the turmeric, cumin, mustard and fennel seeds over a medium heat for about 2 minutes, until the spices smell aromatic. Add to the slow cooker.

3 Add the potatoes to the slow cooker and stir until coated in the spices. Season well with salt and add the tomato purée, tomatoes and yoghurt. Cook for 4 hours on the high setting or 8 hours on low.

4 Serve the potatoes hot with basmati rice.

goan aubergine curry

Aubergines have quite a neutral flavour and are therefore well suited to being paired with many different ingredients. They melt into the crowd here, getting along fine with the hot, sweet and fresh flavours of the curry. Serve this with naan breads to mop up all the delicious juices.

serves **6** • prep time **20 mins** • cooking time **4 hours on high/8 hours on low**

3 aubergines, each cut into 8 pieces
4 tbsp sunflower oil
2 tbsp garlic purée
3 cm piece fresh root ginger, grated
1 onion, sliced
1 green chilli, deseeded and chopped
15 fresh or 30 dried curry leaves

1 tbsp tamarind paste
50 g sweetened desiccated coconut
Salt
6 tomatoes, quartered
4 tbsp chopped coriander
Naan breads, to serve

1 In a dry frying pan over a high heat, sear the aubergine on both sides. Spoon into the slow cooker.

2 Heat the oil over a medium heat in the pan and cook the garlic purée and ginger for about a minute until aromatic. Transfer to the slow cooker.

3 Add the onion, chilli, curry leaves, tamarind paste, coconut and salt. Cook for 4 hours on the high setting or 8 hours on low.

4 About 5 minutes before the end of the cooking time, add the tomatoes.

5 To serve, sprinkle over the coriander leaves and serve with the warmed naan breads.

VEGETARIAN AND VEGETABLE DISHES

greek-style butter bean and potato casserole

This is a beautifully simple dish, but sometimes that is all you want. Serve it with some green vegetables and good bread for a vegetarian supper. If you wanted to add a bit more substance (or humour the meat-eaters), you could stir through some chopped ham or cooked bacon at the end.

serves **6** • prep time **15 mins** • cooking time **4 hours on high/8 hours on low**

4 tbsp olive oil
2 mild Spanish onions, sliced
4 garlic cloves, crushed
200 ml red wine
400 g white potatoes, diced
120 g turnip, thinly sliced

3 x 410 g cans butter beans, drained and rinsed
2 x 400 g cans chopped tomatoes
400 ml vegetable stock
Pinch of paprika
1 bay leaf
4 tbsp chopped flat-leaf parsley

1 Heat half the oil in a large saucepan over a high heat and cook the onions for about 5 minutes. Stir in the garlic and add the red wine. Let it bubble for a few minutes to deglaze the pan. Season and transfer to the slow cooker. Add the potatoes, turnip and butter beans.

2 Add all the remaining ingredients and mix. Season and cook for 4 hours on the high setting and 8 hours on low.

pumpkin in miso

You don't need to bother with peeling a pumpkin – it's hard work and the skin is actually perfectly edible when cooked. Just make sure you give it a good wash before use. Older pumpkins work better for the slow cooker as they will stand up to the longer cooking time and not disintegrate.

serves **6** • prep time **20 mins** • cooking time **4 hours on high/8 hours on low**

2 tbsp groundnut oil
2 red onions, chopped
3 garlic cloves, chopped
40 g ginger, cut into shreds
1 red chilli, deseeded and sliced
25 g coriander, chopped
1.4 kg pumpkin, uncut into wedges
3 tbsp miso paste

1 litre boiling water
2 tbsp soy sauce
1 x 220 g can water chestnuts, drained
100 g aduki beans, soaked in water
  overnight
1 tbsp sesame oil
3 spring onions, sliced, to garnish

1   Heat half the oil over a medium heat in a large frying pan and cook the onions, garlic, ginger and chilli for 3–4 minutes, until softened. Transfer to the slow cooker with half the coriander.

2   Heat the remaining oil over a medium heat in the frying pan and cook the pumpkin and for a minute, until just softened. Transfer to the slow cooker.

3   Add the miso paste to the slow cooker with the boiling water, soy sauce, water chestnuts and beans. Cook for 4 hours on the high setting or 8 hours on low.

4   To serve, add the remaining coriander and the sesame oil, garnish with the spring onions.

red pepper, tomato and cashew nut bake

This is a huge success with vegetarians – a really tasty, moist nut roast, with a smooth yet crunchy texture and lots of flavour. Unlike conventional nut roasts, which can be fiddly and require lots of attention, this one can be left to simmer away in the slow cooker without you having to worry about it. It can be spread on hot toast for lunch, or served hot with a delicious tomato sauce.

serves **6** • prep time **20 mins** • cooking time **4 hours on high/8 hours on low**

4 red peppers, deseeded and
   roughly sliced
1 onion, cut into chunks
4 garlic cloves
2 tbsp olive oil, plus a little extra
   for oiling
300 g cashew nuts
25 g flat-leaf parsley, roughly chopped

150 g mature Cheddar, grated
2 x 400 g cans chopped tomatoes
75 g dried fine white breadcrumbs
1 tsp dried oregano or marjoram
3 eggs, beaten
1 tsp vegetable stock powder
1 tsp English mustard powder
Salt and freshly ground black pepper

1 Preheat the oven to 220°C/Gas 7.

2 Place the peppers, onion and 3 of the garlic cloves on a baking sheet and drizzle with 1 tablespoon of the oil. Roast in the oven for 20 minutes, until golden, turning once or twice.

3 Meanwhile, place the nuts in the oven on a separate baking sheet and roast for 5 minutes, until golden. Let them cool for a few minutes, then set aside a few for the garnish. Place the others in a food processor. Pulse until coarsely chopped and then place in a large bowl.

4 Peel the roasted garlic. Reserve a few of the peppers, and chop the remaining peppers in the food processor with the roasted garlic and onion, the parsley and Cheddar. Drain one of the cans of tomatoes and add to the mixture. Pulse until chopped finely and then add to the nuts.

5 Add the breadcrumbs, oregano, eggs, stock powder and mustard powder to the bowl, season with salt and pepper, and mix well.

6 Lightly oil the slow cooker pot and scatter the base with the reserved peppers and cashew nuts, roughly chopped. Spoon the tomato mixture on top and level the surface. Cook for 4 hours on the high setting or 8 hours on low.

7 Start making the tomato sauce about 40 minutes before the end of the cooking time. Put the remaining can of tomatoes and tablespoon of oil in a saucepan with the last garlic clove (lightly bashed) and place over a low heat. Add seasoning and leave to simmer for 30–40 minutes.

8 Serve the cashew bake hot with the tomato sauce. Alternatively, allow it to cool and serve with freshly toasted slices of bread.

north african chickpea curry with
toasted flatbread

We are now very fortunate to have easy access to spices from all over the world. The ras el-hanout spice mix used here comes from Morocco; it is subtly fragranced with rose petals. There is no definitive combination of spices that makes up ras el-hanout; in Morocco every home cook, shop and food company has their own secret combination of over a dozen spices.

serves **6** • prep time **15 mins** • cooking time **4 hours on high/8 hours on low**

3 tbsp sunflower oil
2 onions, roughly chopped
4 carrots, roughly chopped
4 garlic cloves, chopped
2 green chillies, deseeded and sliced
4 tsp ras el-hanout spice blend
500 ml vegetable stock
3 x 400 g cans chickpeas, rinsed
  and drained

Grated zest and segmented flesh of
  1 lemon
150 g ready-to-eat dried apricots,
  halved
$\frac{1}{2}$ tsp turmeric
3 large tomatoes, roughly chopped
25 g coriander, roughly chopped
Flatbreads, to serve

1 Heat the oil over a high heat in a large frying pan and cook the onions, carrots, garlic and chillies for about 10 minutes, until softened.

2 Add the ras el-hanout and fry for 2 minutes. Then add the remaining ingredients, except the coriander, and bring to a simmer. Transfer to the slow cooker and cook for 4 hours on the high setting or 8 hours on low.

3 About 10 minutes before the end of the cooking time, heat the oven to 200°C/ Gas 6. Slice the flatbreads into large pieces, brush with a little olive oil and place on a baking sheet. Place in the oven for 5–6 minutes, until toasted.

4 To serve the curry, stir through the coriander and divide between warmed plates, with the flatbread served separately.

classic veggie chilli with zingy avocado salsa

This is the ultimate vegetarian chilli – so packed with flavour that you'll never miss the meat. If you're a chilli lover, serve a small dish of thinly sliced chillies or some pickled jalapeños alongside for that extra kick.

serves **4-6** • prep time **20 mins** • cooking time **4 hours on high/8 hours on low**

3 tbsp olive oil
1 aubergine, cut into 2 cm cubes
1 onion, diced
3 garlic cloves, chopped
1 carrot, diced
1 tbsp mild chilli powder
1 tsp ground cumin
1 tsp ground coriander
2 tbsp tomato purée
2 tsp cocoa powder
1 courgette, diced
2 peppers, diced
100 g green beans, cut into 3 cm lengths

400 g can chopped tomatoes
400 g can red kidney beans, drained and rinsed
Pinch of sugar (optional)
Salt and freshly ground black pepper
1 large ripe avocado, peeled, stoned and diced
10 cm piece of cucumber, halved, seeded and finely diced
Few sprigs of coriander, chopped
Few sprigs of mint, chopped
4 spring onions, thinly sliced
Zest and juice of 1 lime

1   Heat 2 tablespoons of the oil in a large frying pan over a high heat, add the aubergine and fry for 5 minutes, stirring, until browned. Transfer to the slow cooker.

2   Add the remaining oil to the frying pan and fry the onion, garlic, carrot and spices for 5 minutes over a medium heat until slightly softened. Stir in the tomato purée and cook for a further minute before adding the cocoa, courgette, peppers, green beans, tomatoes and kidney beans. Allow to heat through then transfer to the slow cooker. Season well, adding a pinch of sugar (if using) and cook for 4 hours on the high setting or 8 hours on low.

3   While the chilli is cooking, make the salsa by mixing together all the ingredients in a serving bowl. Taste and add a little extra lime juice, if you like. Chill until required. Serve the chilli with some rice, baked potatoes or wedges, with the salsa on the side.

mushroom stroganoff
with green peppercorns and herby rice

This is a deliciously 'meaty' non-meat dish. Buy a good mix of mushrooms for this stroganoff, to give it different shapes and colour. Chestnut mushrooms, large flat, portobellini and button are all widely available and equally tasty.

serves **4** • prep time **15 mins** • cooking time **4 hours on high/8 hours on low**

2 tbsp olive oil
15 g butter
2 onions, peeled and thinly sliced
3 garlic cloves, peeled and thinly sliced
2 tsp sweet paprika
1½ tsp green peppercorns in brine, drained and roughly crushed
4 tbsp brandy
150 ml hot strong mushroom or vegetable stock

2 medium waxy potatoes, peeled and cut into 2 cm dice
650 g mixed mushrooms, cut into 2 cm thick slices
250 g white rice
Small bunch of flat-leaf parsley, chopped
Handful of celery leaves
142 ml pot soured cream
Salt and freshly ground black pepper

1   Heat the oil and butter in a large frying pan over a medium heat and brown the onions and garlic. Stir in the paprika and peppercorns and cook for a further minute. Carefully add the brandy and bring it to the boil – watch out, it may flare up – then add the hot stock.

2   Place the potatoes and mushrooms in the slow cooker and pour over the onion mixture. Season, then cook for 4 hours on the high setting or 8 hours on low.

3   About 15 minutes before serving, cook the rice according to the packet instructions, drain, and mix with half the parsley and the celery leaves.

4   Season the stroganoff to taste, then add the soured cream and heat through for a few minutes. Stir in the remaining parsley to serve.

rich provençal sauce for pasta

Slow cookers are invaluable when you want to produce a gutsy, slowly reduced tomato sauce. If you are cooking this dish for non-veggies and want to boost the flavour, add six chopped anchovy fillets before cooking. This is delicious served with buttered fresh tagliatelle.

serves **6** • prep time **15 mins** • cooking time **4 hours on high/8 hours on low**

6 tbsp extra virgin olive oil
6 garlic cloves, finely chopped
200 ml red wine
3 tbsp chopped rosemary
1 bay leaf
75 g 'dry' pitted olives, roughly sliced

3 tbsp capers in brine, drained
2 x 400 g cans plum tomatoes,
 roughly crushed
400 g can artichoke hearts,
 drained and sliced
Salt and freshly ground black pepper

1 Heat the oil in a large frying pan over a medium heat, add the garlic and cook for a few minutes until it softens. Pour in the red wine, increase the heat and boil rapidly until the wine has reduced by two-thirds. Add the remaining ingredients to the pan, bring to a simmer and transfer the sauce to the slow cooker.

2 Season well and cook for 4 hours on the high setting or 8 hours on low.

VEGETARIAN AND VEGETABLE DISHES

pearl barley, butternut squash and sage risotto

A hugely successful flavour combination, butternut squash and sage has become a popular feature on many a good gastro-pub menu. In this recipe the sweet orange flesh of the squash melts into a rich, nutty, pearl barley risotto.

serves **6** • prep time **15 mins** • cooking time **3½ hours on high/7 hours on low**

4 tbsp extra virgin olive oil
1 onion, finely chopped
4 garlic cloves, chopped
2 celery sticks, diced
200 ml white wine
3 tbsp chopped sage leaves
1 bay leaf
1 large butternut squash, peeled, seeded and cut into 3 cm chunks

350 g pearl barley, washed well
1.7 litres hot vegetable stock
75 g finely grated Parmesan or strongly flavoured vegetarian cheese
Large knob of butter
Salt and freshly ground black pepper

1 Heat the oil in a large pan over a medium heat and cook the onion, garlic and celery for 5 minutes until slightly softened. Add the wine, increase the heat and boil for a few minutes until reduced by half. Transfer to the slow cooker.

2 Stir in the sage, bay leaf, squash, barley and stock, season well, cover and cook for 3½ hours on the high setting, 7 hours on low. Stir in the cheese and butter just before serving. If you like a little more bite to your risotto, 3 hours on high, 6 hours on low will be fine.

split pea daal with butter naan

A steaming bowl of chana daal is pure Indian comfort food. It is equally delicious served cold, drizzled with a little olive oil and served with chapati and a crisp salad.

serves **4** • prep time **15 mins, plus soaking** • cooking time **4 hours on high/8 hours on low**

300 g split peas (also called yellow peas or chana daal)
1.2 litres hot vegetable stock
2 tbsp sunflower or olive oil
25 g butter
3 tsp coriander seeds, crushed
1½ tsp cumin seeds, crushed
1 large onion, finely chopped
4 garlic cloves, chopped
1 red and 1 green chilli, thinly sliced

50 g fresh root ginger, peeled and finely chopped
Zest and juice of 1 lemon
25 g coriander, roughly chopped
150 g baby leaf spinach
Salt and freshly ground black pepper
25 g salted butter, at room temperature
Large pinch of chilli powder
1 tbsp finely chopped coriander
2 x 150 g plain cooked naan breads

1 Wash the split peas and leave to soak in cold water for 8 hours, or overnight. Drain and place in a large saucepan, cover with the stock and bring to the boil. Simmer for 15 minutes, skimming off any foam with a spoon, then transfer to the slow cooker.

2 In a large frying pan, heat the oil and butter then add the coriander, cumin, onion, garlic, chillies and ginger and cook for 5 minutes until the onion is soft. Transfer to the slow cooker, season well and cook for 4 hours on the high setting or 8 hours on low.

3 About 5 minutes before the end of cooking, check the seasoning then stir in the lemon zest and juice, fresh coriander and spinach leaves. Allow to heat through.

4 For the naan, preheat the grill to medium. Mix together the butter, chilli powder and coriander. Sprinkle both sides of each naan with water and place them under the grill, bottom-side up, for 2 minutes. Turn, spread with the spiced butter and grill for a further 1–2 minutes until golden and bubbling. Serve straight away with the daal.

thai green curry with pan-fried tofu

Making your own Thai curry paste from scratch requires patience and a lot of ingredients, so you might think it's not worth the efffort; especially when you taste this delicious recipe, whch uses good-quality bought paste!

serves **4** • prep time **15 mins** • cooking time **4 hours on high/8 hours on low**

3 tbsp sunflower or groundnut oil
200 g shallots, peeled and sliced
3 garlic cloves, chopped
3 tbsp good-quality bought Thai green curry paste
2 fresh or dried kaffir lime leaves
1 tsp palm sugar or light muscovado sugar
400 g can coconut milk
150 ml hot vegetable stock
2 tsp Thai fish sauce (omit for vegetarians)

600 g waxy potatoes, peeled and cut into 3 cm chunks
2 carrots, peeled, halved lengthways and cut thickly on the diagonal
2 peppers, roughly chopped
150 g green beans, halved
150 g baby corn
250 g firm tofu, cut into 3 cm cubes
250 g bok choi, leaves separated
3 tbsp roughly chopped coriander
Lime wedges, to serve

1 Heat 2 tablespoons of the oil in a medium frying pan over a high heat, add the shallots and garlic and cook for 5 minutes until golden. Stir in the curry paste, lime leaves and sugar and cook for a minute until aromatic. Pour in the coconut milk, stock and fish sauce (if using) and bring to the boil.

2 Place the potatoes in the slow cooker followed by the carrots, peppers and green beans. Pour over the hot liquid, scatter the corn on top and cook for 4 hours on the high setting or 8 hours on low.

3 About 10 minutes before the end of the cooking time, heat the remaining oil in the frying pan over a high heat, add the tofu and fry until golden. Stir into the curry with the bok choi and coriander and leave for 2 minutes until the leaves have wilted. Serve the curry scattered with coriander and with some lime wedges alongside to squeeze over for a little extra zing!

red pepper falafel bake

If you're anything like me and find sesame-crusted falafel hard to resist, you are sure to love this falafel-inspired loaf. Filled with the classic flavours of cumin, coriander and tahini, it makes a great slow-cooker dish. Serve it warm or chilled with the yoghurty dip and some crisp salad leaves.

serves **4-6** • prep time **25 mins** • cooking time **5 hours on high/10 hours on low**

1 tbsp coriander seeds
2 tsp cumin seeds
465 g jar roasted red peppers in brine, drained
2 x 400 g cans chickpeas, drained
3 garlic cloves, crushed
4 tbsp tahini paste
3 tbsp extra virgin olive oil
Juice of 1 lemon
2 tbsp toasted sesame seeds

50 g fresh white breadcrumbs
100 g spring onions, finely sliced
4 tbsp roughly chopped coriander
Salt and freshly ground black pepper
15 cm piece cucumber, halved and seeded
150 g natural yoghurt
1 tbsp tahini paste
2 tbsp chopped dill
Squeeze of lemon juice

1 Toast the coriander and cumin seeds in a small frying pan over a medium heat until aromatic, then transfer to a pestle and mortar and grind until coarse. Pat the peppers dry on kitchen paper, then cut into 1 cm dice.

2 In a food processor, put three-quarters of the chickpeas, the garlic, tahini, olive oil and lemon juice. Pulse until coarse, then scoop into a bowl and mix in the ground spices with the peppers, sesame seeds, breadcrumbs, spring onions and coriander. Season well.

3 Spoon everything into a well-oiled slow cooker, smooth the surface, scatter with the reserved chickpeas and cook for 5 hours on the high setting or 10 hours on low.

4 For the dip, coarsely grate the cucumber then squeeze out the juice between your hands. Transfer to a bowl and combine with the yoghurt, tahini, dill and some lemon juice to taste. Serve alongside the falafel bake.

porcini mushroom and ale casserole
with thyme dumplings

If you're searching for the ultimate comfort food for the colder months, look no further than a hearty casserole with dumplings. Choose a paler-coloured ale, as darker varieties can be too bitter once cooked, and be sure to buy an extra bottle to serve at the table!

serves **4** • prep time **25 mins, plus 20 minutes soaking** • cooking time **4 hours on high/8 hours on low**

15 g dried porcini mushrooms
2 tbsp olive oil
16 shallots, peeled and halved
3 carrots, cut into chunks
3 celery sticks, sliced
25 g butter
350 g chestnut mushrooms, halved
300 ml light ale
2 tbsp fresh chopped thyme
2 bay leaves
1 tbsp wholegrain mustard

3 tbsp mushroom ketchup
300 ml hot mushroom or vegetable stock
2 tsp cornflour
Salt and freshly ground black pepper

For the dumplings
200 g self-raising flour
1 tsp English mustard powder
100 g salted butter, chilled
1 tbsp chopped thyme
1 tbsp finely chopped parsley

1 Place the porcini mushrooms in a bowl, cover with 100 ml boiling water and leave to soak for 20 minutes. Remove the mushrooms, drain briefly and roughly chop. Strain the soaking liquid through a sieve lined with kitchen paper and set aside.

2 Heat the oil over a medium-high heat in a large frying pan, add the shallots, carrots and celery and cook for 5 minutes until tinged brown. Spoon into the slow cooker. Add the butter to the pan, increase the heat, add the porcini and chestnut mushrooms, season well and cook for 5 minutes until golden. Transfer everything to the slow cooker.

3 Pour the ale into the frying pan and boil rapidly for a few minutes until reduced by half. Add the herbs, mustard, mushroom ketchup, stock and the reserved mushroom liquor. Bring to a simmer, and pour into the slow cooker.

4 Mix the cornflour with 2 tablespoons cold water in a small bowl until smooth, then add to the casserole and stir. Cook for 4 hours on the high setting or 8 hours on low.

5 About 40 minutes before the end of the cooking time, make the dumplings. Sieve the flour and mustard into a large bowl and season well. Coarsely grate the cold butter into the flour, dipping it into the flour to prevent sticking. Add the herbs and rub in the butter until the texture resembles coarse breadcrumbs. Add 6–8 tablespoons cold water a tablespoon at a time, mixing with a table knife to combine, until you have a soft, lightly sticky dough. Cut into 8 portions and shape into balls. Drop onto the casserole, cover, and continue to cook for 30 minutes or until the dumplings have a light springiness.

creamy italian white bean and fennel stew

The distinctive aniseed flavour of fennel always makes me think of the Mediterranean and this Italian-inspired dish is no exception. I've added mascarpone to this stew to add a little naughtiness to an otherwise super-healthy dish!

serves **4** • prep time **20 mins** • cooking time **3 hours on high/6 hours on low**

2 tbsp olive oil
15 g butter
1 large sweet onion, peeled and diced
4 garlic cloves, chopped
2 celery sticks, thinly sliced
400 g turnips, peeled and cut into
  2 cm cubes
3 medium fennel bulbs, cut into large
  wedges, fronds removed and set aside
  for garnish

2 x 400 g cans cannellini or haricot
  beans, drained
75 ml dry vermouth or white wine
2 sprigs of rosemary, leaves only
2 bay leaves
400 ml hot vegetable stock
100 g mascarpone cheese
Crusty bread, to serve
Salt and freshly ground black pepper

1 Heat the oil and butter in a large frying pan and cook the onion, garlic, celery, turnip and fennel wedges until light golden, then transfer to the slow cooker.
Add the beans, vermouth, herbs and stock. Season well and cook for 3 hours on the high setting or 6 hours on low.

2 At the end of the cookting time, place the mascarpone in a bowl, spoon in some of the hot cooking liquor and blend until smooth. Pour the mixture into the slow cooker, add the reserved fennel fronds, stir, then serve with crusty bread.

swede, jerusalem artichoke and chestnut hotpot

It's a shame, but Jerusalem artichokes are often overlooked as a winter vegetable. However, once you've tried them in this dish, teamed with rich chestnuts and juicy swede, you'll be digging out the recipe books for other ways to serve them.

serves **4** • prep time **20 mins** • cooking time **4 hours on high/8 hours on low**

25 g butter
1 tbsp sunflower oil
1 onion, sliced
1 leek, sliced into 1cm rounds
2 celery sticks, sliced
1 medium swede, peeled and cut into
   3 cm chunks
500 g Jerusalem artichokes, scrubbed
   well and halved if large

2 tbsp chopped thyme
2 bay leaves
Freshly grated nutmeg, to taste
500 ml hot vegetable stock
200 g vacuum-packed, cooked,
   peeled chestnuts
Salt and freshly ground black pepper

1 Melt the butter and oil in a large frying pan over a medium–high heat, add the onion, leek, celery and swede and fry for about 10 minutes until golden brown. Transfer to the slow cooker with the remaining ingredients.

2 Season well and cook for 4 hours on the high setting or 8 hours on low. Serve with crusty bread.

waldorf loaf

Inspired by the classic salad, this meatloaf-style loaf makes a comforting winter meal served with mashed or roast potatoes and buttered greens, or a satisfying summer dish served cold with crusty bread, a peppery-leaved salad and a glass of chilled white wine.

serves **6** • prep time **20 mins** • cooking time **2 hours on high/5 hours on low**

2 tbsp olive oil
6 shallots, peeled and finely chopped
1 tbsp thyme leaves
4 sprigs of rosemary, leaves finely
   chopped
100 ml dry white wine
1 large carrot, peeled and coarsely
   grated
1 eating apple, cored and chopped

2 tsp English mustard powder
1 tbsp sherry vinegar
100 ml hot vegetable stock
200 g walnut pieces
3 celery sticks, cut into small dice
125 g fresh wholemeal breadcrumbs
200 g Stilton or other hard blue cheese,
   crumbled
Salt and freshly ground black pepper

1 Heat the oil in a large frying pan over a medium heat and cook the shallots, thyme and rosemary until golden. Add the wine and boil rapidly until very little liquid remains. Stir in the carrot, apple and mustard powder and cook for 2 minutes. Pour in the vinegar and stock and heat through.

2 Meanwhile, blend 150 g of the walnuts in a food processor until coarse and tip out into a bowl. Roughly chop the remaining walnuts and add to the bowl along with the celery and breadcrumbs. Mix in the cooked ingredients, season well, then spoon into a well-buttered slow cooker.

3 Cook for 2 hours on the high setting or 5 hours on low. Leave to cool, uncovered, for 15 minutes before serving.

chickpea and paneer curry with cool salsa

Pan-fried paneer (Indian cheese) makes this curry a really substantial yet healthy meal. Paneer is available from most good supermarkets and specialist shops, but if you can't get it, hard-boiled eggs make an equally delicious substitute.

serves **6** • prep time **15 mins** • cooking time **4 hours on high/8 hours on low**

3 tbsp sunflower oil
2 medium onions, thinly sliced
4 garlic cloves, chopped
1 red chilli, finely chopped
6 cardamom pods, seeds only, roughly crushed
1 tsp ground turmeric
5 tsp garam masala
2 tsp fennel seeds
1 large potato, about 300 g, peeled and diced

2 x 400 g cans chickpeas, drained
500 g pot natural yoghurt
3 tbsp mango chutney
450 g paneer, cut into 3 cm cubes
Salt and freshly ground black pepper
Zest and juice of 2 limes
2 tbsp chopped coriander
2 tbsp chopped mint
3 medium ripe tomatoes, seeded and finely chopped
1 shallot, finely chopped

1 Heat 2 tablespoons of the oil in a large frying pan over a medium heat and cook the onions, garlic, chilli and spices until deep golden. Transfer to the slow cooker and stir in the potato, chickpeas, yoghurt and mango chutney.

2 Season well and cook for 4 hours on the high setting or 8 hours on low. Meanwhile, heat the remaining oil in the frying pan, add the paneer and cook for about 5 minutes, stirring often until it turns a deep golden brown. Remove from the pan and set aside, then stir it into the curry 10 minutes before the end of the cooking time.

3 For the salsa, mix together the lime zest and juice, coriander, mint, tomatoes and shallot. Season well and allow to stand at room temperature for an hour to allow the flavours to infuse. Serve alongside the curry.

smoky chipotle black bean chilli tacos

This chilli ticks all the boxes for an informal meal for friends or a speedy family supper. It's cheap and hassle-free to make, rich and smoky, and really healthy too! It's also perfect as a topping for a fluffy baked potato.

serves **4** • prep time **10 minutes** • cooking time **4 hours on high/8 hours on low**

3 tbsp olive oil
1 large red onion, finely chopped
6 garlic cloves, chopped
1 tsp chipotle chilli paste
1 tsp smoked paprika
1 bay leaf
600 g fresh ripe tomatoes, roughly
    chopped

2 x 400 g cans black beans, drained
    and rinsed
3 tbsp chopped coriander
12 taco shells, to serve
200 g soured cream, to serve
200 g medium Cheddar, grated, to serve
Salt and freshly ground black pepper

1   Heat the oil in a large frying pan and fry the onion and garlic for 5 minutes on a medium heat until softened. Add the chilli paste, paprika and bay leaf and cook for a further minute. Stir in the tomatoes, then transfer everything to the slow cooker.

2   Season well, stir in the beans and cook for 4 hours on the high setting or 8 hours on low. Stir through the coriander once cooked.

3   To serve, place the chilli on the table and allow everyone to fill their tacos with chilli and a spoonful of soured cream and cheese. (As an optional extra you could also serve shredded iceberg lettuce and diced cucumber.)

moorish potato and cauliflower stew

In this stew, fragrant and sweet aromatic spices turn two humble vegetables into a really special dish. Crush your potatoes a little on the plate to soak up all the vibrant broth, and use a spoon to scoop up every last tasty drop!

serves **4–6** • prep time **20 mins** • cooking time **3 hours on high/6 hours on low**

3 tbsp olive oil
1 large sweet onion, peeled and
    roughly chopped
2 garlic cloves, sliced
600 g baby (bite-sized) new potatoes,
    scrubbed
2 tsp coriander seeds, ground
2 tbsp tomato purée
5 cm piece cinnamon stick
Large pinch of saffron

1 large celery stick, sliced
1 medium cauliflower, about 500 g,
    broken into florets
75 g sultanas
400 g can butterbeans, drained
700 ml hot vegetable stock
3 large fresh tomatoes, peeled, seeded
    and chopped
40 g flaked almonds, toasted

1 Heat the oil in a large frying pan over a medium heat and cook the onion, garlic and potatoes for 4–5 minutes until tinged brown. Add the coriander seeds and tomato purée and cook for a further minute, stirring.

2 Place the cinnamon, saffron, celery, cauliflower, sultanas and butterbeans in the slow cooker. Stir in the onion and potato mixture and pour over the stock. Check the seasoning then cook for 3 hours on the high setting or 6 hours on low.

3 Before serving, stir through the tomatoes and scatter each individual portion with toasted almonds.

sweet and sour vegetable noodles

If you're put off by the luminous colour of take-away sweet and sour dishes, this easy-to-cook home-made version will be a welcome alternative. The natural flavours of the vegetables are enhanced by zingy citrus tones and delicate spices.

serves **4** • prep time **20 mins** • cooking time **3 hours on high/6 hours on low**

1 tbsp sunflower oil
1 large onion, thickly sliced
100 g cashew nuts
2 carrots, halved lengthways and sliced thickly on the diagonal
2 celery sticks, sliced
4 garlic cloves, chopped
30 g fresh root ginger, peeled and cut into matchsticks
Pinch of chilli flakes
1 star anise
1 green and 1 red pepper, thickly sliced
225 g can water chestnuts

4 tbsp rice wine vinegar
4 tbsp mirin, rice wine or dry sherry
2 tbsp caster sugar
Juice of 1 lemon
125 ml pineapple juice
2 tbsp cornflour
1 tbsp sesame oil
600 g cooked egg noodles
150 g mangetout, halved
8 spring onions, thinly sliced on the diagonal
Salt and freshly ground black pepper

1 Heat the oil in a large frying pan over a high heat and cook the onion for 2 minutes. Add the cashews, carrots, celery, garlic and ginger and cook for a further 2–3 minutes until tinged with brown. Transfer to the slow cooker and scatter over the chilli flakes, star anise, peppers and water chestnuts.

2 In a small bowl, combine the vinegar, mirin or rice wine or sherry, sugar, lemon juice, pineapple juice and cornflour until smooth. Season well and pour the sauce into the slow cooker. Cook for 3 hours on the high setting or 6 hours on low.

3 About 10 minutes before the end of the cooking time, stir in the sesame oil, noodles and mangetout and continue to cook. Serve spooned into bowls and topped with the spring onions.

pardina lentil bolognese

If you want a few simple pasta sauces in your repertoire, this one is sure to become a family favourite. As it cooks your kitchen will fill with a mouthwatering herby, tomatoey aroma that will call everyone to the table without you needing to!

serves **6** • prep time **20 mins** • cooking time **4 hours on high/8 hours on low**

6 tbsp extra virgin olive oil
2 red onions, finely chopped
6 garlic cloves, chopped
1 large carrot, diced
2 celery sticks, diced
2 courgettes, diced
100 g tomato purée
2 x 400 g cans chopped tomatoes

200 g pardina lentils
300 ml vegetable stock
2 bay leaves
40 g basil, roughly chopped
1½ tsp dried oregano
1 tbsp thick balsamic vinegar
1 tsp granulated or caster sugar
Salt and freshly ground black pepper

1   Heat the oil in a large frying pan over a medium heat, then add the vegetables and cook for 5 minutes until lightly softened, but not coloured. Add the tomato purée and cook for 2 minutes. Add all the remaining ingredients, reserving about a third of the basil, season well, and bring to a simmer.

2   Transfer to the slow cooker and cook for 4 hours on the high setting or 8 hours on low. Stir through the remaining basil before serving with your favourite pasta, or use the sauce to make a delicious lasagne.

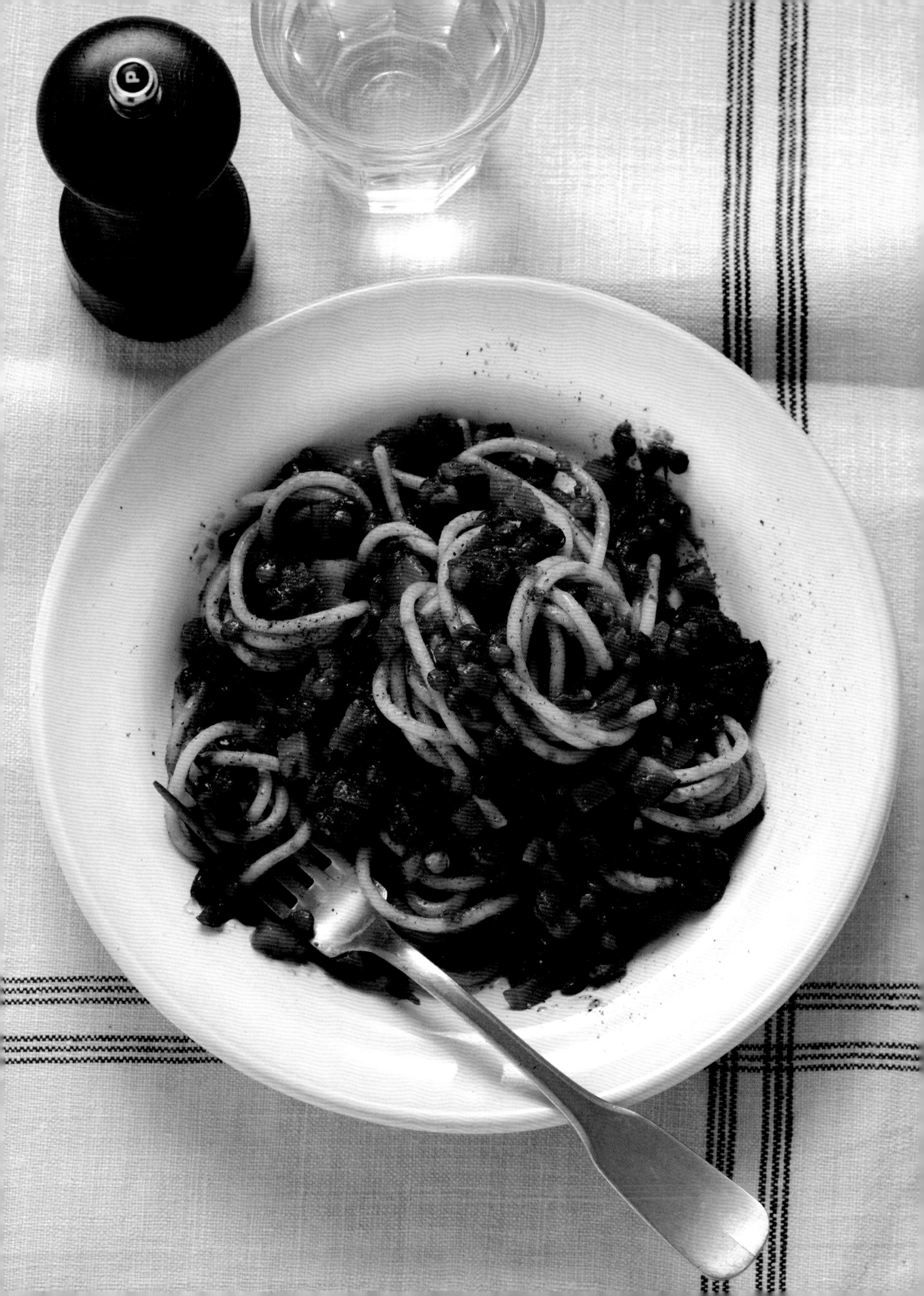

COOKING
FOR FRIENDS

creamy chicken and mushroom

If you're entertaining friends midweek, you want a recipe that's simple to cook, welcoming, and suits all tastes. This is the perfect dish for sharing; delicately flavoured, creamy and inviting, it will get everyone talking.

serves **6** • prep time **15 mins** • cooking time **4 hours on high/8 hours on low**

2 tbsp sunflower or olive oil
30 g butter
2 onions, chopped
2 carrots, peeled and chopped
500 g boneless, skinless chicken
   thighs, diced
2 tbsp plain flour
2 tsp garlic salt
300 ml hot chicken stock

300 ml milk
1 bay leaf
2 large sprigs of thyme
300 g mushrooms, larger ones
   quartered
Salt and freshly ground black pepper
250 g long grain rice, to serve
3 tbsp chopped flat-leaf parsley,
   to serve

1 Heat half the oil and butter in a large frying pan over a medium heat and cook the onions and carrots for 2 minutes. Transfer to the slow cooker.

2 Heat the remaining oil in the frying pan over a high heat and cook the chicken until it is sealed all over. Spoon the chicken into the slow cooker and stir in the flour and garlic salt. Pour over the stock and milk and some black pepper. Add the bay leaf and thyme and cook for 4 hours on the high setting or 8 hours on low.

3 About 15 minutes before the end of the cooking time, cook the rice according to the packet instructions and stir the mushrooms into the chicken. Garnish with the parsley and serve hot over the rice.

chicken tikka masala

This perennial favourite works very well in the slow cooker. Set it to cook before you head off to work on Friday morning and you can return home to restorative curry with pickles, poppadums and cold beer.

serves **6** • prep time **20 mins** • cooking time **4 hours on high/8 hours on low**

1.5 kg chicken pieces
2 tbsp oil
2 onions, chopped
120 ml coconut milk
400 g can chopped tomatoes
120 ml natural low-fat yoghurt
1 tsp cornflour
3 tbsp tomato purée
1 tbsp cumin seeds
2 tsp garam masala
1 tbsp black onion seeds
5 cm piece of fresh root ginger, chopped

3 tbsp freshly squeezed lemon juice
2 garlic cloves, chopped
2 tsp cayenne pepper, or to taste
1 red chilli, chopped
15 g mint, chopped
15 g coriander, chopped
Lime wedges, to serve
350 g basmati rice, to serve
Naan bread, to serve
Raita, to serve

1   Heat the oil in a large frying pan over a high heat and brown the chicken pieces all over. Transfer to the slow cooker.

2   Heat the remaining oil in the frying pan over a high heat and cook the onions for 5 minutes. Set aside. Add the coconut milk and tomatoes to the slow cooker. Mix the yoghurt with the cornflour and stir this in too.

3   Using a blender or food processor, blend the fried onion with the rest of the ingredients up to and including the chilli. Add to the slow cooker and cook for 4 hours on the high setting or 8 hours on low.

4   Just before serving, cook the rice according to the packet instructions. Stir the mint and coriander into the curry and serve hot with the rice, naan bread and some raita on the side.

chicken tagine
with baby aubergines, coriander and sumac

Baby aubergines are easy to find in ethnic stores and some supermarkets and are well worth searching out, as their mild heat and pepperiness adds a lot of flavour to dishes. Sumac is a spice mix that is becoming increasingly popular and available – look out for it in the supermarket or deli.

serves **6** • prep time **15 mins** • cooking time **4 hours on high/8 hours on low**

1.5 kg chicken pieces
4 tbsp olive oil
2 onions, chopped
2 carrots, chopped
5 baby aubergines, halved
2 garlic cloves, left whole
1 cinnamon stick
1 bay leaf

1 tbsp sumac powder
1 lemon, sliced
200 ml hot chicken stock
400g can chopped tomatoes
400 g couscous, to serve
30 g coriander, chopped to serve
Natural yoghurt, to serve
Salt and freshly ground black pepper

1 Season the chicken. Heat the oil in a large frying pan over a medium heat and cook the chicken until golden. Transfer to the slow cooker.

2 Heat the remaining oil in the frying pan over a medium heat and brown the onions, carrots, aubergines and garlic. Stir in the cinnamon, bay leaf, sumac, lemon, stock and tomatoes. Transfer to the slow cooker and cook for 4 hours on the high setting or 8 hours on low.

3 Just before serving, prepare the couscous according to the packet instructions. Stir the coriander into the tagine and serve hot over the couscous with the natural yoghurt in a small serving bowl.

tandoori chicken

Another Indian classic; I think this is just as nice cold for a casual weekend lunch, with a bit of salad and fresh bread, as it is served hot with the traditional accompaniments. The ultimate mood food!

serves **6** • prep time **10 mins** • cooking time **4 hours on high/8 hours on low**

50 g butter
1 tbsp cayenne pepper
2 garlic cloves, crushed
1 tbsp garam masala
1 tbsp coriander seeds, crushed
1 onion, finely chopped
2 kg chicken

1 lemon, chopped
1 red onion, chopped
Coriander, to garnish
Lemon wedges, to serve
Raita, to serve
Naan bread, to serve
Salt and freshly ground black pepper

1 Use a pestle and mortar or a food processor to blend together the butter, cayenne, garlic, garam masala, coriander seeds, onion and seasoning.

2 Take the chicken and pat dry with kitchen paper. Use a small sharp knife to make slashes in the breast, thigh and drumsticks. Rub the spice paste into the chicken, pushing well into the flesh where you have cut it with the knife.

3 Put the lemon and red onion in the base of the slow cooker and set the chicken on top. Cover and cook for 4 hours on the high setting or 8 hours on low.

4 Serve hot or cold with the lemon wedges, raita and naan bread on the side.

Note: Suitable for a 6 litre model; for the 3 litre size, use a 1.2 kg chicken

jalapeño chicken with tacos

I think of this as match food – if the football is on, or any other sporting competition – this is perfect fodder for excited fans. Lay it out on a table and get your friends to help themselves before they settle in front of the tv.

serves **6** • prep time **15 mins** • cooking time **4 hours on high/8 hours on low**

3 tbsp olive oil
2 red onions, chopped
2 green peppers, chopped
4 garlic cloves, chopped
3 tbsp tomato purée
1 tsp paprika
2 tsp ground cinnamon
1 tbsp coriander seeds, crushed
50 g jalapeño chillies, chopped

1 tsp fresh lemon juice
400 g can blackeye beans, drained
1.5 kg chicken pieces
1 tbsp plain flour
Iceberg lettuce, chopped, to serve
Guacamole, to serve
Taco shells, to serve
Salt and freshly ground black pepper

1 In the slow cooker, mix half the oil with the onions, peppers, garlic, tomato purée, paprika, cinnamon, coriander seeds, chillies, lemon juice, beans and seasoning.

2 Heat the remaining oil in a large frying pan over a medium heat and fry the chicken until golden all over. Season well and stir in the flour. Spoon into the slow cooker and cook for 4 hours on the high setting or 8 hours on low.

3 Serve the chicken hot with the iceberg lettuce and guacamole for stuffing into the tacos.

butter-basted whole chicken with
lemon and thyme

When chicken is cooked this way, it is succulent and full of flavour remaining moist even when cooked. Try serving it at room temperature in the warmer months with a crunchy selection of summer vegetables.

serves **8** • prep time **10 mins** • cooking time **4 hours on high/8 hours on low**

50 g butter
Juice and zest of 1 lemon
2 tbsp thyme leaves
1 x 2 kg chicken
150 ml chicken stock
3 tbsp cornflour

2 tbsp chopped parsley (optional)
Salt and freshly ground black pepper
Sugar snap peas, to serve
Baby carrots, to serve
Mangetout, to serve

1 Mash together the butter, lemon juice and zest, thyme and salt and pepper. Using your fingers, push the butter in between the skin and breast of the chicken or rub it all over the chicken breast.

2 Place the chicken in the slow cooker and pour the stock into the bottom. Cover and cook for 4 hours on the high setting or 8 hours on low.

3 Remove chicken from the cooker and set aside to keep warm while you make the sauce.

4 To make the sauce, spoon off the excess fat from the cooking liquid and place the remaining juices in a pan over a medium heat. Mix the cornflour in a cup with a little water and then stir into the gravy together with the parsley, if using, and bring to a simmer to thicken. Simmer for 3–4 minutes, to cook the cornflour and allow the flavours to mellow, before serving with the chicken and vegetables.

spanish chicken with olives

Large family gatherings mean many and varied tastes and needs, and I find that this hits the spot every time. You can serve the chicken with a variety of partners – garlic bread, shredded greens, broccoli or rice – but my favourite is sautéed potatoes, which I explain how to cook in this recipe.

serves **6** • prep time **15 mins** • cooking time **4 hours on high/8 hours on low**

10 tbsp olive oil
1.5 kg part-boned chicken breasts and
   chicken thighs, skin on
1 tbsp plain flour
2 mild onions, chopped
2 red peppers, deseeded and chopped
4 garlic cloves, chopped
3 tbsp tomato purée

1 tsp paprika
4 tbsp chopped flat-leaf parsley
100 ml red wine
100 g pitted black olives
1 x 400 g can chopped tomatoes
Salt and freshly ground black pepper
2 kg waxy potatoes, diced

1 Heat 3 tablespoons of the olive oil in a large frying pan over a medium heat. Meanwhile, season the chicken and cook in the oil for about 5 minutes, until golden. Transfer the chicken to the slow cooker and stir in the flour.

2 Heat a further 3 tablespoons olive oil in the frying pan over a medium heat and cook the onions, peppers and garlic for about 5 minutes, until softened. Stir in the tomato purée, paprika, parsley and red wine, then add to the chicken and season. Add the olives and the chopped tomatoes to the slow cooker. Cook for 4 hours on the high setting or 8 hours on low.

3 About 30 minutes before the end of the cooking time, cook the potatoes. Heat the remaining olive oil over a medium heat in a large frying pan, and add the potatoes (you might have to fry them in batches or use two pans). Sauté for 15 minutes, until cooked through. Season with salt and keep warm if you are cooking in batches.

4 Serve the chicken on warmed plates accompanied by the sautéed potatoes.

coq au vin

This French staple comes from Burgundy, using the red wine that is added liberally to all dishes from that area. Coq au vin has the added bonus of being much improved on reheating, which means that you can make it the day before, and simply reheat when you are ready.

serves **6** • prep time **15 mins** • cooking time **4 hours on high/8 hours on low**

4 tbsp olive oil
1.6 kg chicken, jointed into 8–10 pieces, skin on
6 tbsp plain flour
200 g shallots
250 g Chantenay carrots, trimmed
2 onions, chopped
500 ml red wine
100 ml brandy

4 rosemary sprigs
3 thyme sprigs
2 bay leaves
200 g smoked streaky bacon, each rasher cut into three
500 ml chicken stock
Salt and freshly ground black pepper
2 kg waxy potatoes, diced, to serve
Flat-leaf parsley, to serve

1 Heat 3 tablespoons of the olive oil in a large frying pan over a medium heat. Meanwhile, season the chicken and cook in the oil for about 5 minutes, until golden. Transfer the chicken to the slow cooker and stir in the flour.

2 Heat the remaining oil in the frying pan over a medium heat and cook the shallots, carrots and onions for 10 minutes, or until softened. Stir in the wine, brandy, rosemary, thyme, bay leaves and seasoning. Simmer for 10 minutes, or until reduced by half.

3 In a separate dry pan, brown the bacon, then add to the slow cooker.

4 Add the cooked vegetables to the chicken, pour in the hot stock and stir well. Cook for 4 hours on the high setting or 8 hours on low.

5 Steam the diced potatoes in a saucepan for about 10 minutes, or until tender. To serve, place the chicken pieces on a serving plate, spoon over the sauce and serve with the steamed potatoes, garnished with flat-leaf parsley.

piripiri chicken

Slow cooking is perfect for parties, as the dishes can generally be kept warm easily and guests can eat when they like. To feed a crowd, double this recipe, hold back on the chillies and serve it with a chilli sauce for those hardier souls. It's great with a vodka cocktail.

serves **6** • prep time **15 mins** • cooking time **4 hours on high/8 hours on low**

4 tbsp olive oil
1.5 kg chicken thighs and drumsticks, skin on
1 tbsp plain flour
2 red peppers, deseeded and chopped
2 green peppers, deseeded and chopped
2 onions, chopped
4 garlic cloves, crushed

3 tbsp tomato purée
1 red chilli, deseeded and chopped
1 green chilli, deseeded and chopped
1 tbsp chilli powder
2 tsp ground cinnamon
2 bay leaves
Juice and zest of 2 lemons
Salt and freshly ground black pepper
Long grain white rice, to serve

1 Heat half the olive oil in a frying pan over a medium heat. Meanwhile, season the chicken pieces and then cook in the oil for about 5 minutes, until they are golden. (You might have to cook them in batches.) Transfer the chicken to the slow cooker and stir in the flour.

2 Heat the remaining oil over a medium heat in the frying pan and cook the red and green peppers, onions and garlic for about 5 minutes, until softened. Add seasoning and stir in the tomato purée, red and green chillies, chilli powder, cinnamon and bay leaves. Continue cooking for 1–2 minutes, until the spices smell aromatic. Transfer the contents of the pan to the slow cooker.

3 Add the lemon juice and zest. Cover and cook for 4 hours on the high setting or 8 hours on low. Serve on plates or in large bowls, spooned over the cooked long grain rice.

mexican baked chicken with pinto beans

This is perfect for a filling family feast. Mexican food is very sociable: there are generally lots of accompaniments to the main dish, which means there is a lot of helping yourself, and passing backwards and forwards across the table. Everyone can load up their plates with the accompaniments they like most, which means that the more robust, spicier flavours can be left to the adventurous diners.

serves **6** • prep time **15 mins** • cooking time **4 hours on high/8 hours on low**

1.5 kg part-boned chicken breasts and
   chicken thighs, skin on
4 tbsp sunflower oil
2 tbsp tomato purée
1 tsp ground coriander
½ tsp ground cinnamon
1 tsp paprika
2 onions, chopped
3 garlic cloves, chopped
2 carrots, chopped

2 green peppers, deseeded and diced
1 x 400 g can chopped tomatoes
2 x 400 g cans pinto beans, drained
   and rinsed
2 tbsp sliced green pimentos in brine
Salt and freshly ground black pepper
6 wheat tortillas, to serve
Sour cream, to serve
Lime wedges, to serve

1 Season the chicken. Heat half the oil over a high heat in a frying pan and cook the chicken for about 5 minutes, until browned all over. Stir in the tomato purée, coriander, cinnamon and paprika, then transfer the mixture to the slow cooker.

2 Heat the remaining oil over a medium heat in the frying pan and cook the onions, garlic, carrots and peppers for about 5 minutes, until softened. Add to the slow cooker together with the chopped tomatoes, pinto beans and pimentos. Cook for 4 hours on the high setting or 8 hours on low.

3 Warm the wheat tortillas in a dry pan and spoon some Mexican baked chicken onto each one. Serve immediately, offering the sour cream and lime to be added before the tortillas are rolled up.

sweet and sour chicken

Even quite young children like the familiar sweet and salty flavours of this dish. It can be enjoyed by all ages, and made into a special feast with the addition of ready-made prawn crackers, sesame toast and spring rolls.

serves **6** • prep time **15 mins** • cooking time **4 hours on high/8 hours on low**

900 g boneless chicken thighs
2 tbsp cornflour
4 tbsp tomato ketchup
4 tbsp sugar
2 tbsp sunflower oil
3 garlic cloves, chopped
2 onions, sliced
1 red pepper, deseeded and
    roughly chopped

1 green pepper, deseeded and
    roughly chopped
2 carrots, sliced
5 tbsp rice wine or white wine vinegar
2 tbsp soy sauce
Salt and freshly ground black pepper
Long grain rice, to serve

1 Put the chicken pieces in a bowl, add seasoning and toss in the cornflour. In a separate bowl, mix together the tomato ketchup and sugar and add 50 ml water.

2 Heat half the oil in a large open pan over a medium heat, add the garlic, onions, peppers and carrots and stir-fry for about 3 minutes. When just golden around the edges, transfer to the slow cooker.

3 Heat the remaining oil over a high heat in the pan and cook the chicken until browned all over. Add the tomato ketchup mix to the pan and stir together well.

4 Transfer the mixture to the slow cooker and cook for 4 hours on the high setting or 8 hours on low. Serve over a bed of cooked rice.

sri lankan chicken curry

Once you have tried a southern Indian or Sri Lankan curry, I guarantee that you too will be converted to their distinctive flavours. These curries are fresh and light and always leave me wanting to return to them. They have no buttery sauces or heavy creamy textures, yet they still taste great with a beer on a Friday night, served simply with rice or chappatis. (Note: jaggery is an unrefined dark sugar sold in blocks.)

serves **6** • prep time **20 mins** • cooking time **4 hours on high/8 hours on low**

4 tbsp sunflower oil
1.8kg chicken thighs and drumsticks, skin on
400 g shallots, sliced
8 garlic cloves, crushed
5 cm piece fresh root ginger, grated
3 green chillies, deseeded and sliced
2 cinnamon sticks
2 tsp ground turmeric
40 g coriander, leaves reserved for garnish and stems chopped

2 tsp jaggery, palm or dark brown soft sugar
15 fresh or 30 dried curry leaves
1.2 litres chicken stock
100 g creamed coconut
2 limes, quartered
Salt
Rice or chappatis, to serve

1 Heat half the oil over a high heat in a frying pan. Season the chicken pieces and brown them all over, cooking in batches if necessary. Transfer to the slow cooker.

2 Heat the remaining oil over a medium heat in the frying pan and cook the shallots for about 5 minutes, until softened. Stir in the garlic, ginger, chillies, cinnamon, turmeric and chopped coriander stems and cook for a further minute, until aromatic. Transfer the shallots and spices to the slow cooker, and also add the jaggery, curry leaves, stock, creamed coconut and limes. Season well with salt. Cover and cook for 4 hours on the high setting or 8 hours on low.

3 Before serving, stir in the reserved coriander leaves. Serve piping hot over rice or with chappatis.

jerk chicken casserole

Plantains are widely available, and although they look like big green bananas, they cannot be eaten raw. The best way to eat them is to slice and fry them – as described in the recipe below.

serves **6** • prep time **15 mins** • cooking time **4 hours on high/8 hours on low**

2 tbsp plain flour
4 tbsp jerk seasoning
1.8kg chicken, jointed into 8–10 pieces, skin on
6 tbsp sunflower oil
2 white onions, chopped
2 celery sticks, chopped
2 green peppers, deseeded and chopped
2 garlic cloves, chopped

2 bay leaves
2 tbsp dark brown soft sugar
2 tbsp rum
1 tbsp red wine vinegar
100 ml chicken stock
Salt and freshly ground black pepper
2 plantain, thickly sliced on the diagonal
1 red chilli, deseeded and chopped, to garnish
Coriander leaves, to garnish

1 Mix together the flour and jerk seasoning and season with salt and pepper. Add the chicken pieces to the mixture, coating thoroughly.

2 Heat 2 tablespoons of the oil in a frying pan over a high heat. Add the chicken and cook for about 5 minutes, until browned all over. Transfer to the slow cooker.

3 Heat a further 2 tablespoons of the oil in the frying pan over a medium heat and cook the onions, celery and green peppers for about 10 minutes, until softened. Stir in the garlic and bay leaves and then add the sugar, rum, vinegar and stock. Transfer all the ingredients to the slow cooker and cook for 4 hours on the high setting or 8 hours on low.

4 Heat the remaining oil over a high heat and fry the plantain for 2 minutes, until golden. (You might have to do this in batches.) Drain on kitchen paper and keep warm. Serve the casserole with the plantain, garnished with the red chilli and coriander.

slow-roast duck with apples

The simple flavours in this dish are rich and intensely satisfying, and the fruity combination of apple and orange is a great success. It's a real taste of the English countryside; ideal for a lazy lunch or dinner after an autumnal walk.

serves **6** • prep time **15 mins** • cooking time **4 hours on high/8 hours on low**

6 duck legs, excess fat removed
2 tbsp plain flour
250 ml cider
1 tbsp olive oil
2 carrots, chopped
400 g shallots, peeled
Zest pared in one piece from 1 orange

300 ml hot chicken stock
4 tbsp chopped thyme
450 g Granny Smith apples, chopped
12 tbsp cider vinegar
Salt and freshly ground black pepper
80 g watercress, to garnish

1 Season the duck legs and fry in a large, dry frying pan over a high heat. Drain on kitchen paper then put in the slow cooker. Stir in the flour.

2 Deglaze the frying pan with the cider and pour the liquid into the slow cooker.

3 Heat the oil in the frying pan over a medium heat and cook the carrots and shallots for a few minutes until golden. Add to the slow cooker with the orange zest, stock, thyme, apples and cider vinegar. Cook for 4 hours on the high setting or 8 hours on low.

4 Serve garnished with watercress.

chinese-style duck in plum sauce

Duck in a piquant oriental sauce is a favourite combination. If you want to stick with tradition, you can shred the duck and serve on pancakes with cucumber and spring onions. Alternatively, you can simply serve the duck over rice, as here.

serves **6** • prep time **15 mins** • cooking time **4 hours on high/8 hours on low**

4 duck legs, skin on
1 tbsp cornflour
1 bunch spring onions, sliced
200 ml Chinese rice wine
3 garlic cloves, chopped

200 ml chicken stock
2 tbsp soy sauce
150 g plum sauce
Freshly ground black pepper
Long grain rice, to serve

1 Place a dry frying pan over a medium to high heat until hot. Add the duck legs, and cook, skin side down, for about 10 minutes, until some fat has rendered and the skin is golden. Discard the fat and set aside the duck legs to cool for 5 minutes.

2 Dust the duck with the cornflour and place in the slow cooker. Add the spring onions.

3 In a saucepan over a medium heat, bring the Chinese wine, garlic, chicken stock, soy sauce and plum sauce to the boil, reduce the heat and leave to simmer for 10 minutes, until all the flavours have mixed together. Season with freshly ground black pepper and add to the slow cooker. Cook for 4 hours on the high setting or 8 hours on low.

4 Serve the duck steaming hot over a bed of rice.

duck with orange, cranberry and thyme

Duck is a popular choice for entertaining and this delicious dish takes advantage of the cheaper leg cut. It's made very attractive by the cranberries in the sauce, and, once garnished with watercress, could almost be passed as restaurant food!

serves **6** • prep time **15 mins** • cooking time **4 hours on high/8 hours on low**

6 duck legs, skin on
2 tbsp cornflour
150 ml orange juice
Rind pared in one piece from 1 orange
75 g dried cranberries
300 ml chicken stock
2 tbsp thyme, chopped
400 g shallots

250 ml fino sherry
200 g small turnips, quartered
Salt and freshly ground black pepper
2 kg Maris Piper or similar potatoes,
   quartered, to serve
4 tbsp olive oil
80 g watercress, to garnish

1 Season the duck legs and then pan fry 3 of them in a dry pan over a high heat for 5 minutes. Drain on kitchen paper and transfer to the slow cooker then do the same with the remaining 3 legs.

2 In a small bowl, mix the cornflour to a paste with the orange juice and set aside.

3 In a separate bowl, mix together the orange rind, cranberries, chicken stock, thyme, shallots, sherry, turnips and seasoning and spoon over the duck. Stir in the cornflour paste. Cook for 4 hours on the high setting or 8 hours on low.

4 About 1 hour before you want to serve your meal, preheat the oven to 200°C/Mark 6. Put the potatoes into a pan of salted water, bring to the boil, then drain immediately. Put into a roasting tin, drizzle over the olive oil, season with a little salt and roast for 20 minutes.

5 Garnish the duck with watercress and serve with the roast potatoes.

lamb shanks with redcurrant and rosemary

Once you have a good lamb shank recipe in your repertoire, you will find reason to cook it time and again. The sauce in this recipe is rich and flavoursome; all you need add is some mashed potato to mop up the juices.

serves **6** • prep time **30 mins** • cooking time **4 hours on high/8 hours on low**

6 lamb shanks, dusted with a little plain
   flour
3 tbsp sunflower oil
200 ml red wine
1 leek, chopped
2 onions, cut into wedges
6 small turnips, quartered
250 g Chantenay carrots, trimmed
700 g small new potatoes
6 rosemary sprigs, finely chopped

3 bay leaves
1.3 litres hot lamb or beef stock
1 tbsp Dijon mustard
5 tbsp redcurrant jelly
1 tbsp red wine vinegar
300 g French green beans
3 tbsp chopped parsley
Salt and freshly ground black pepper
Mashed potato, to serve

1 Season the lamb shanks. Heat 2 tablespoons of the oil over a high heat in a large frying pan, and cook the lamb for about 10 minutes, until browned all over. Transfer to the slow cooker. While the pan is still hot, add the red wine, bring to the boil, then simmer for a few minutes to drive off the alcohol. Add to the slow cooker.

2 Heat the remaining oil over a medium heat in the frying pan and cook the leek, onions, turnips, carrots and potatoes for 10 minutes. Add these to the slow cooker together with the rosemary, bay leaves, stock, mustard, redcurrant jelly and red wine vinegar. Add seasoning and cook for 4 hours on the high setting or 8 hours on low.

3 About 15 minutes before the end of the cooking time, add the green beans to the slow cooker. After 5 minutes, add the parsley. If you are planning to cook and hold this dish, cook the green beans separately and stir them into the dish with the parsley just before serving. Serve the lamb shanks piping hot with the mashed potato.

lamb and lentil curry

This is a lovely, easy, hearty curry that will create a warm glow around the table. The addition of lentils means you need less meat, which makes this dish easy on the purse, too.

serves **6** • prep time **15 mins** • cooking time **4 hours on high/8 hours on low**

1.2 kg lamb, diced
2 tbsp oil
2 onions, chopped
4 garlic cloves, crushed
5 cm piece of fresh root ginger, finely
  grated
1 tbsp crushed dried chillies
1 tsp fennel seeds (optional)
1 tbsp coriander seeds

1 tbsp cumin seeds
100 g green lentils
500 ml hot lamb stock
500 g tomato passata
1 bay leaf
4 tbsp roughly chopped coriander,
  to serve
Cooked basmati rice, to serve
Salt and freshly ground black pepper

1 Season the lamb. Heat half the oil in a large frying pan over a high heat and brown the lamb well all over. Transfer to the slow cooker.

2 Heat the remaining oil in the frying pan and cook the onions, garlic and ginger over a medium heat for 5 minutes until softened. Stir in the bay leaf, chillies, fennel (if using), coriander and cumin seeds and season well. Transfer everything to the slow cooker and add the lentils, stock and passata. Cook for 4 hours on the high setting or 8 hours on low.

3 Serve hot, garnished with the fresh coriander and accompanied by the rice.

greek-style lamb with feta and parsley

This is one of my favourite recipes; the potatoes magically absorb the full flavour of the lamb, and the feta adds a deliciously contrasting texture and taste to the dish. Perfect for a lazy Sunday lunch in the summer sun.

serves **6** • prep time **15 mins** • cooking time **4 hours on high/8 hours on low**

1 kg lamb shoulder, diced
3 tbsp chopped rosemary
2 onions, quartered
1 head garlic, cut in half horizontally
4 tomatoes, halved
500 g waxy potatoes, peeled and
  thickly sliced
100 ml white wine

200 ml hot chicken stock
100 ml olive oil
200 g feta cheese, crumbled
50 g flat-leaf parsley, roughly chopped
Grated zest and juice of 1 lemon
5 tbsp olive oil
Salt and freshly ground black pepper

1 Season the lamb. Put the rosemary, onions, garlic, tomatoes and potatoes in the slow cooker and place the lamb on top.

2 Pour over the wine, hot stock and 100 ml oil and cook for 4 hours on the high setting or 8 hours on low.

3 Combine the feta cheese, parsley, lemon zest and juice and olive oil and stir through the lamb just before serving.

lamb and pea curry

Peas are a great addition to a curry, as they provide fresh flavour and bump up the vegetable content – and I always seem to have a bag of peas in the freezer! This simple dish needs no more than some warm naan bread to mop up the juices, Indian pickles, such as lime or aubergine, and a cool raita to accompany it.

serves **6** • prep time **20 mins** • cooking time **4 hours on high/8 hours on low**

1.2 kg minced lamb
2 tbsp oil
2 onions, chopped
2 garlic cloves, crushed

3 tbsp medium curry powder
300 ml hot lamb stock
300 g tomato passata

1   Season the lamb. Heat half the oil in a large frying pan over a high heat and brown the lamb well. Transfer to the slow cooker.

2   Heat the remaining oil in the frying pan over a medium heat and cook the onions and garlic for about 2 minutes until softened. Stir in the curry powder. Transfer the pan contents to the slow cooker, add the stock and passata and cook for 4 hours on the high setting or 8 hours on low.

3   Serve hot, with your preferred accompaniments.

lamb biryani

An aromatic, mild curry; the fragrant flavours in the sauce gently pervade the rice. Using brown rice makes the dish extra healthy, and basmati is ideal for those who are not keen on plain brown, as it has a more subtle texture.

serves **6** • prep time **15 mins** • cooking time **3 hours on high/6 hours on low**

6 tbsp vegetable or sunflower oil
1 kg lamb shoulder, diced
2 onions, chopped
3 garlic cloves, chopped
5 cm piece of fresh root ginger, chopped
1 bay leaf
2 tsp coriander seeds, crushed
2 tsp cumin seeds
1 tsp chilli flakes
200 g brown basmati rice, washed

2 tbsp tomato purée
100 ml coconut milk
100 ml natural yoghurt
300 ml hot lamb stock
25 g mint, chopped
25 g coriander, chopped
6 spring onions, finely sliced
Mango chutney, to serve
Salt and freshly ground black pepper

1 Heat half the oil in a frying pan over a high heat and brown the lamb. Season well and transfer to the slow cooker.

2 Heat the remaining oil in the frying pan over a medium heat and fry the onions, garlic, ginger, bay leaf, coriander seeds, cumin seeds, and chilli flakes for 2 minutes until the spices are aromatic and the onion is softened. Mix in the rice, transfer to the slow cooker and stir in the tomato purée.

3 Pour over the coconut milk, yoghurt and stock and cook for 3 hours on the high setting or 6 hours on low.

4 Just before serving, combine the mint, coriander and spring onions and sprinkle the mix over the biryani. Offer the mango chutney alongside for guests to help themselves to.

pot-roasted gammon in cider with apples

This is a beautifully sweet dish, with the sharpness of the apples mellowed out into the sauce. Mashed potato makes the perfect accompaniment.

serves **6** • prep time **20 mins** • cooking time **4 hours on high/8 hours on low**

1 kg unsmoked gammon joint, soaked
   overnight in cold water and drained
25 g butter
1 leek, diced
1 onion, diced
1 stick celery, diced
1 carrot, diced

2 Granny Smith apples, cut into wedges
   and cored
200 ml pork or chicken stock
300 ml cider
2 tbsp mustard powder
2 bay leaves
Salt and freshly ground black pepper
Mashed potato, to serve

1 Put the gammon in a colander in the sink and pour a kettle of boiling water over the joint.

2 Melt the butter over a medium heat in a saucepan and cook the diced vegetables for about 5 minutes, until softened. Add seasoning, then transfer the vegetables to the slow cooker and add the apples, stock, cider and mustard. Tuck the bay leaves under the gammon strings.

3 Add the gammon joint to the slow cooker, nestling it down among the vegetables. Cook for 4 hours on the high setting or 8 hours on low.

4 To serve, drain the slow-cooked sauce into a saucepan and boil for about 5 minutes to reduce by a half. Slice the gammon thinly and serve with the vegetables from the broth and mashed potato.

ham hock with boston baked beans

Ham hock is a cheap cut of meat, widely available at good butchers. You might not be able to specify the weight, as hocks often come vacuum packed, but the recipe is very forgiving and will taste good however much you have. The ham hock is very tasty, but also quite fatty and, like a lot of flavoursome cuts, long cooking draws out the full flavour.

serves **6** • prep time **20 mins** • cooking time **4 hours on high/8 hours on low**

1 tbsp sunflower oil
2 onions, chopped
2 carrots, chopped
5 garlic cloves, chopped
1 ham hock, about 450 g
2 x 400 g cans chopped tomatoes
2 x 420 g cans pinto beans, drained and rinsed
2 x 420 g cans kidney beans, drained and rinsed
2 x 420 g cans butterbeans, drained and rinsed

2 tbsp Dijon mustard
2 tbsp tomato purée
300 ml chicken or vegetable stock
1 tsp paprika
50 g dark muscovado sugar
3 tbsp black treacle
2 tsp ground cinnamon
3 tbsp Worcestershire sauce
Salt and freshly ground black pepper
Green vegetables, to serve
Cornbread, to serve

1 Heat the oil over a high heat in a frying pan and cook the onions, carrots and garlic for about 5 minutes, until softened. Spoon into the slow cooker.

2 Add all the remaining ingredients to the slow cooker and cook for 4 hours on the high setting or 8 hours on low.

3 At the end of the cooking time, remove the ham hock from the stew and slice the meat off the bone.

4 Serve the sliced ham with the beans and cornbread next to it.

braised gammon with polenta crust

serves **6–8** • prep time **20 mins** • cooking time **4 hours on high/8 hours on low**

1.6 kg unsmoked gammon joint, soaked
  overnight in water
6 tbsp olive oil
2 rosemary sprigs
3 garlic cloves, unbashed
450 ml boiling water

1 tsp finely chopped rosemary
1 tsp finely chopped parsley
50 g instant polenta
Salt and freshly ground black pepper
1 kg tomatoes, halved, to serve
Crusty bread, to serve

1 Drain the gammon, rinse in fresh water and pat dry with kitchen paper. Using a sharp knife, remove the rind from the gammon, then season the joint with freshly ground black pepper. Heat 1 tablespoon of the oil over a high heat in a large saucepan and seal the gammon all over.

2 Wrap the gammon in foil, putting the rosemary sprigs and garlic inside the parcel. Put into the slow cooker, and pour in 250 ml of the boiling water and 2 tablespoons of the olive oil. Cook for 4 hours on the high setting or 8 hours on low.

3 About 30 minutes before the end of the cooking time, preheat the oven to 200°C/ Mark 6. Put the tomatoes into a baking tray, season with salt and pepper and roast for 15 minutes until softened.

4 Start making the polenta about 15 minutes before the end of the cooking time. Put the remaining 200 ml of boiling water in the saucepan with the chopped rosemary, parsley, a pinch of salt and the remaining 3 tablespoons of olive oil. When the water is boiling, pour in the polenta in a thin stream so that the water does not stop boiling. Stir constantly for about 3 minutes, until all the liquid has been absorbed. Set the polenta aside to cool, then break up with a fork until quite crumbly.

5 Spread the polenta out on a baking sheet. When the gammon is cooked, discard the rosemary and garlic cloves and roll in the polenta, pressing the crumbs into the meat.

6 Slice and serve warm with the roasted tomatoes and crusty bread. It is delicious served cold too. Simply wrap in cling film tightly to keep the crumb in place and cool.

braised pork with caramelised leeks

Pork and leek is a combination that never fails; the sweetness of leeks perfectly enhances the flavour of pork. In this recipe, the juices of the braised meat are transformed into a rich sauce with the addition of a little double cream.

serves **4** • prep time **20 mins** • cooking time **4 hours on high/8 hours on low**

1 kg pork shoulder, diced
4 tbsp olive oil
2 onions, chopped
2 carrots, chopped
4 garlic cloves, chopped
3 tbsp thyme leaves, chopped
1 bay leaf
100 ml hot chicken stock

200 ml cider
100 ml double cream
30 g butter, to serve
2 leeks, finely sliced, to serve
2 tbsp demerara sugar, to serve
Mashed potato, to serve
Sea salt and freshly ground
  black pepper

1 Season the pork. Heat half the oil in a frying pan over a high heat and brown the pork on all sides. Spoon into the slow cooker.

2 Heat the remaining oil in the frying pan over a medium heat and soften the onions, carrots and garlic. Spoon into the slow cooker.

3 Add the thyme, bay leaf, stock, cider and cream. Mix well, season and cook for 4 hours on the high setting or 8 hours on low.

4 About 10 minutes before serving, heat the butter in a frying pan over a medium heat and cook the leeks, stirring often, until really soft and golden. Stir in the sugar and, when melted, remove from the heat.

5 Serve the pork, garnished with the leeks, over mashed potato.

slow-roasted chinese-style pork ribs

If you love Chinese food but are put off making it because of the lists of ingredients or variety of dishes on offer, try this simple recipe. The mellow and sweet flavours of the Chinese ingredients tease out the rich flavours of the pork, and through long slow cooking they all meld together in a rich and piquant sauce. Once you've tried this, you won't rush for the Chinese take-away menu again!

serves **6** • prep time **15 mins** • cooking time **4 hours on high/8 hours on low**

4 tbsp finely grated fresh root ginger
3 garlic cloves, crushed
1 tbsp chilli flakes (optional)
200 ml hoisin sauce
4 tbsp clear honey
50 ml rice wine or mirin

1.5 kg pork spare ribs
1 tbsp sesame oil
300 g cooked long grain rice, to serve
3 eggs, beaten, to serve
2 spring onions, chopped, to serve

1 Combine the ginger, garlic, chilli flakes (if using) hoisin sauce, honey and rice wine in a large bowl. Add the pork and mix until the sauce coats the spare ribs evenly. Add everything to the slow cooker and cook for 4 hours on the high setting or 8 hours on low.

2 About 5 minutes before the end of the cooking time, heat the sesame oil over a high heat in a wok or large frying pan and add the cooked rice. Stir and toss for 2 minutes, until the rice is heated through, then add the beaten egg and spring onions and stir until combined.

3 Serve the spare ribs with the sauce poured over and accompanied by the egg-fried rice.

beef in tomato and basil

Basil is available in supermarkets throughout the year, but is best in summer, when it is in season; this is when its flavour is strongest and its aniseed notes, which complement the strong flavours of the beef, most pronounced.

serves **6** • prep time **15 mins** • cooking time **4 hours on high/8 hours on low**

800 g stewing steak or shin of beef, diced
4 tbsp olive oil
2 onions, diced
2 carrots, diced
2 rosemary sprigs, leaves only
4 garlic cloves
200 ml Italian red wine

200 ml hot beef stock
2 tbsp tomato purée
500 g tomato passata
Pinch of sugar
4 tbsp basil leaves, torn
Extra virgin olive oil, to serve
Pasta of your choice
Parmesan shavings, to serve

1 Season the beef. Heat half the oil in a large frying pan over a high heat and cook the beef until well browned all over. Spoon into the slow cooker.

2 Heat the remaining oil in a frying pan over a medium heat and brown the onions and carrots. Chop the rosemary and garlic together, so that the flavours combine, and stir into the pan. Pour on the wine, let it bubble a bit, then transfer everything to the slow cooker.

3 Add the stock, tomato purée, passata and sugar then cook for 4 hours on the high setting or 8 hours on low.

4 Just before serving, cook the pasta according to the packet instructions and stir the basil and a glug of oil through the beef.

5 Serve hot with pasta and pass around the Parmesan separately.

spicy beef with chipotle sauce and coriander

Mexican food is perfect for sharing with friends at an informal supper, not least because it can be stretched to include unexpected guests by adding accompaniments. This is a lovely Tex-Mex dish bursting with colour, flavour and texture. Rinsing the chillies gives the sauce a nice rounded heat without that sense of burning.

serves **6** • prep time **15 mins** • cooking time **4 hours on high/8 hours on low**

2 tbsp olive or sunflower oil
1.4 kg stewing steak, diced
1 carrot, roughly diced
2 green peppers, roughly diced
3 red onions, roughly chopped
3 garlic cloves, crushed
100 ml hot beef stock
4 tbsp tomato purée
3 tbsp mild chilli powder

2 tbsp chilli flakes
3 spring onions, chopped
$\frac{1}{2}$ cucumber, peeled, seeded
  and diced
100 g natural yoghurt
50 g soured cream
Handful of coriander leaves, to serve
250 g long grain rice, to serve
Salt and freshly ground black pepper

1 Heat 1 tablespoon of oil in a large frying pan over a high heat and cook the beef until well browned. Transfer to the slow cooker.

2 Add the remaining oil to the frying pand and cook the carrot, green peppers and onions for a few minutes until softened. Add to the slow cooker with the garlic, stock, tomato purée and chilli powder. Season well and cook for 4 hours on the high setting or 8 hours on low.

3 Combine all the chilli sauce ingredients in a bowl and set aside until ready to eat.

4 Just before serving, cook the rice according to the packet instructions. Serve the spicy beef over the rice, scattered with coriander and accompanied by the chilli sauce.

Note: Suitable for the 3 litre model, the recipe can be doubled for larger models

meatball casserole with tomato sauce

Meatballs are always popular, enjoyed by young and old alike, and this is a delicious way of allowing all the lovely flavours to develop in a rich sauce. I don't always use egg when forming meatballs, but they need it when cooked in a slow cooker, otherwise they will fall apart.

serves **6** • prep time **20 mins** • cooking time **4 hours on high/8 hours on low**

400 g minced beef
400 g minced pork
1 egg, beaten
4 tbsp olive oil
1 onion, chopped
2 carrots, chopped
3 garlic cloves, chopped
1 celery stalk, chopped

1 tbsp tomato purée
100 ml red wine
2 x 400 g cans chopped tomatoes
1 tbsp mixed herbs
1 tsp sugar
Sea salt and freshly ground
    black pepper

1 Mix together the beef, pork, egg and seasoning in a large bowl. Divide the mixture into 12 and shape each piece into a meatball. They don't have to be perfect, but try to get them as compact as you can.

2 Heat half the oil in a large frying pan over a high heat and seal the meatballs, cooking them until golden brown all over. Transfer to the slow cooker.

3 Heat the remaining oil in the frying pan and cook the onion, carrots, garlic and celery for 5 minutes until softened. Transfer to the slow cooker. Stir in the tomato purée, red wine, chopped tomatoes, mixed herbs, sugar and seasoning. Cook for 4 hours on the high setting or 8 hours on low.

4 Serve hot, with pasta, if you wish.

steak and ale casserole

This is a warm-hearted and welcoming stew, perfect when the weather outside is chilly and uninviting! It is also one of the most rewarding recipes to cook in a slow cooker. The firm stewing steak gradually breaks down over lengthy cooking to produce a velvety textured sauce and succulent meat.

serves **6** • prep time **15 mins** • cooking time **4 hours on high/8 hours on low**

1.4 kg stewing steak, diced
50 g butter or sunflower spread
2 tbsp plain flour
300 ml hot beef stock
1 bay leaf
1 large sprig of thyme
3 onions, diced

3 carrots, diced
2 celery stalks, diced
200 ml ale or beer
1 tsp English mustard
4 tbsp chopped curly parsley
Seasonal green vegetables, to serve

1 Season the beef. Heat half the butter or sunflower spead in a large frying pan over a high heat and cook the beef in batches until well browned. Spoon into the slow cooker and stir in the flour.

2 Pour a little of the stock into the frying pan and use a wooden spoon to scrape off any residue. Transfer to the slow cooker with the bay leaf and thyme. Heat the remaining butter or sunflower spread and cook the onions, carrots and celery over a medium heat until softened. Add to the slow cooker with the remaining stock, the beer and mustard. Stir well.

3 Cook for 4 hours on the high setting or 8 hours on low.

4 Serve hot with green vegetables of your choice.

beef stroganoff

Beef, cream, sweet peppers and garlic in a delicious mix of flavours, with texture and taste – and just a little spicy warmth. What's not to like?

serves **6** • prep time **15 mins** • cooking time **4 hours on high/8 hours on low**

1.4 kg stewing steak, diced
2 tbsp sunflower oil
200 ml red wine
100 ml beef stock
3 onions, sliced
3 red peppers, deseeded and sliced
3 garlic cloves, crushed
4 tbsp tomato purée

1 tbsp paprika
2 tbsp Dijon mustard
300 g field mushrooms, wiped
  and quartered
100 ml crème fraîche
Salt and freshly ground black pepper
375g brown rice, to serve

1   Season the steak. Heat half the oil over a high heat in a large frying pan and cook the beef for about 10 minutes, until browned all over.

2   Add the red wine and stock and, once simmering, pour the beef and liquid into the slow cooker.

3   Heat the remaining oil over a medium heat in the pan and cook the onions, red peppers and garlic for about 5 minutes, until softened. Stir in the tomato purée, paprika and Dijon mustard. Season with salt and freshly ground black pepper.

4   Transfer to the slow cooker and stir in the mushrooms. Cook for 4 hours on the high setting or 8 hours on low.

5   To serve, stir the crème fraîche through the stroganoff, and spoon over the hot brown rice.

beef and guinness casserole
with colcannon mash

serves **8** • prep time **30 mins** • cooking time **4 hours on high/8 hours on low**

1 kg stewing steak, diced
½ tsp cayenne pepper
4 tbsp sunflower oil
150 g butter
600 ml beef stock
250 g streaky bacon, each rasher cut into three
400 g carrots, cut into large chunks
4 onions, roughly chopped
2 celery sticks, chopped
50 g plain flour
3 bay leaves
3 tbsp chopped thyme
200 ml Guinness
2.5 kg Maris Piper potatoes, chopped
Salt and freshly ground black pepper
1 cabbage, chopped, to serve

1 Season the beef with a little salt and cayenne pepper. Heat half the oil and 50 g of the butter in a large frying pan over a high heat and cook the beef, in batches if necessary, until browned all over. This will take about 15 minutes. Spoon into the slow cooker.

2 Pour a little of the stock into the pan and use a wooden spoon to scrape off any residue. Add to the slow cooker.

3 Heat the remaining oil and 50 g more of the butter in the pan over a medium heat and cook the bacon, carrots, onions and celery for about 10 minutes, until softened. Transfer to the slow cooker. Stir in the flour and then add the bay leaves, thyme, Guinness and remaining stock. Cook for 4 hours on the high setting or 8 hours on low.

4 Start making the mash about 25 minutes before the end of the cooking time. Put the potatoes into a saucepan of water. Bring to the boil, reduce to a simmer and cook for 20 minutes, until tender. Meanwhile, steam the cabbage over boiling water for about 10 minutes, until very tender. Drain the potatoes, reserving some of the liquid. Add some of the potato water and the remaining butter to the pan and mash the potatoes thoroughly until no lumps are left. Add seasoning and stir in the cabbage.

5 Serve the colcannon mash with the hot casserole.

slow-cooked oxtail with brown lentils

Oxtail needs slow, leisurely cooking for all of the flavours to blend and mellow. For this reason, it has become the kind of dish usually seen only in restaurants and gastropubs. But when canny slow cooks ask at the butcher they will be pleasantly surprised to find that oxtail is easily available, and at quite low cost.

serves **6** • prep time **15 mins** • cooking time **4 hours on high/8 hours on low**

1.2 kg oxtail, cut into pieces
50 g plain flour
4 tbsp butter
200 g brown lentils
2 onions, chopped
2 carrots, chopped
2 celery sticks, chopped
2 tbsp tomato purée

2 tsp anchovy essence
1 bay leaf
2 tbsp chopped parsley
2 tbsp chopped thyme
500 ml beef stock
Salt and freshly ground black pepper
Steamed potatoes, to serve

1 Season the oxtail and toss it in the flour. Heat half the butter over a high heat in a large frying pan and cook the oxtail for about 10 minutes, until well browned all over (you might have to do this in batches). Spoon it into the slow cooker together with the brown lentils.

2 Heat the remaining butter over a medium heat in the pan and cook the onions, carrots and celery for about 10 minutes, until softened. Transfer to the slow cooker and stir in the tomato purée, anchovy essence, bay leaf, parsley and thyme.

3 Add the stock and season well. Cook for 4 hours on the high setting or 8 hours on low.

4 Serve the oxtail hot with the steamed potatoes.

beef and chorizo casserole with salsa

I like to serve this hearty casserole with something equally robust, such as potato wedges (see page 100). It can also be served with tortilla wraps for some tasty help-yourself fajitas.

serves **8** • prep time **15 mins** • cooking time **4 hours on high/8 hours on low**

1.4 kg stewing steak, diced
2 tbsp plain flour
3 tbsp sunflower oil
2 mild onions, roughly chopped
250 g chorizo, diced
2 garlic cloves, crushed
400 ml beef stock
1 x 400 g can chopped tomatoes
1 x 300 g can pinto or borlotti beans, drained and rinsed

Large pinch of chilli flakes
1 tsp chopped thyme
3 tbsp tomato purée
2 ripe avocados, stoned and chopped
Juice of 2 limes
4 tbsp chopped coriander
Salt and freshly ground black pepper
Tortilla wraps, to serve

1 Toss the steak in the flour to coat. Heat 1 tablespoon of the oil over a high heat in a large frying pan and cook half the beef for about 5 minutes, until well browned all over. Transfer to a plate and repeat with the rest of the steak.

2 Heat the remaining oil over a medium heat in the pan and cook the onions for a few minutes, until softened. Then add the chorizo and cook for a few more minutes.

3 Add the stock, chopped tomatoes, pinto (or borlotti) beans, chilli flakes, thyme, tomato purée and seasoning. Return the beef to the pan and bring to a simmer. Transfer to the slow cooker and cook for 4 hours on the high setting or 8 hours on low.

4 Start making the potato wedges about 30 minutes before the end of the cooking time (see step 4, page 100).

5 For the salsa, stir together the avocados, lime juice and coriander and add seasoning. Serve alongside the casserole and potato wedges.

beef provençal with olives and anchovies

Salty anchovies cook down in the rich beef sauce here, making it piquant but not remotely 'fishy'.

serves **6** • prep time **15 mins** • cooking time **4 hours on high/8 hours on low**

1 kg beef shin, diced
2 tbsp plain flour
3 tbsp olive oil
175 g streaky bacon, each rasher cut
  into three
30 g anchovies in olive oil, drained
  and chopped
250 g carrots, roughly chopped
350 g small onions, quartered
200 ml full-bodied red wine
100 ml brandy
6 garlic cloves

2 beef tomatoes, chopped
100 g pitted black olives
2 bay leaves
3 parsley sprigs, roughly chopped
1 tbsp oregano
1 piece orange rind, peeled with a
  vegetable peeler
500 ml beef stock
Salt and freshly ground black pepper
Macaroni, rigatoni or penne pasta,
  to serve

1 Dust the beef with flour. Heat 2 tablespoons of the oil over a high heat in a large frying pan and cook half the beef for about 5 minutes, until evenly browned. Transfer to the slow cooker. Repeat the process using the remaining beef and oil.

2 Add the bacon to the pan, reduce the heat to medium and cook for a few minutes, until coloured. Stir in the anchovies and then transfer to the slow cooker.

3 Add the carrots and onions to the pan and cook for about 10 minutes, until softened, then transfer to the slow cooker. Finally, add the wine and brandy to the pan and boil rapidly for a few minutes to deglaze it and drive off the alcohol. Pour into the slow cooker with all the remaining ingredients. Cook for 4 hours on the high setting or 8 hours on low.

4 Just before serving cook the pasta according to the packet instructions, drain and return to the hot pan. Toss in the butter and serve with the beef Provençal.

tuscan braised beef in chianti

Beans are widely enjoyed in Italy, and one of the most popular is the borlotti bean. It has a soft texture, but retains a firmness after long cooking, and gives a savoury flavour with no hint of bitterness. The borlotti beans in this dish provide an interesting contrast in texture to the beef.

serves **6** • prep time **15 mins** • cooking time **4 hours on high/8 hours on low**

800 g stewing steak or shin of beef, diced
8 tbsp olive oil
2 onions, diced
2 carrots, diced
1 rosemary sprig
4 garlic cloves, peeled
350 ml Chianti wine
200 ml beef stock

2 tbsp tomato purée
2 x 400 g cans borlotti beans, drained and rinsed
A pinch of sugar
1 x 400 g can tomatoes, drained
Salt and freshly ground black pepper
2.5 kg potatoes, diced, to serve
4 tbsp chopped flat-leaf parsley

1   Season the beef. Heat 2 tablespoons of the oil in a large frying pan over a high heat and cook the beef for 10 minutes, until browned all over. Spoon into the slow cooker.

2   Heat another 2 tablespoons of the oil over a medium heat in the pan and cook the onions and carrots for about 10 minutes, until softened. Chop the rosemary and garlic together so that the flavours meld, and stir into the pan. Pour in the wine, bring to a simmer for about 2 minutes and transfer to the slow cooker.

3   Add the stock, tomato purée, borlotti beans, sugar and tomatoes. Cook for 4 hours on the high setting or 8 hours on low.

4   About 30 minutes before the end of the cooking time, preheat the oven to 200°C/Gas 6. In a baking tin, toss the potatoes in the remaining 4 tablespoons of oil and season well. Roast for 30 minutes.

5   Serve the Tuscan beef with the roast potatoes and sprinkle all with the parsley.

beef and cashews with coconut and chilli

This dish is inspired by the flavours of Malaysia. The spices are sweetly aromatic and, unlike Thai or Vietnamese cuisine, the sauces are made rich by the addition of nuts. To really enjoy these flavours, serve over rice noodles and toss the sauce through to coat them all over.

serves **6** • prep time **15 mins** • cooking time **4 hours on high/8 hours on low**

600 g braising beef, sliced
2 tbsp cornflour
2 tbsp sunflower oil
2 red peppers, deseeded and sliced
2 onions, sliced
3 garlic cloves, chopped
100 ml soy sauce
50 ml rice wine
2 tbsp peanut butter

200 ml chicken stock
200 g cashews, toasted
100 g baby corn
Salt and freshly ground black pepper
600 g rice noodles, to serve
Spring onions, to garnish
Green chilli, deseeded and sliced,
   to garnish
Fresh coconut, shaved, to garnish

1   Season the beef and dust with the cornflour. Heat half the oil over a high heat in a large frying pan and cook the beef for about 5 minutes, until browned all over. Transfer to the slow cooker.

2   Heat the remaining oil over a medium heat in the pan and cook the peppers, onions and garlic for about 5 minutes, until softened. Transfer to the slow cooker.

3   In the same pan, heat together the soy sauce, rice wine, peanut butter and stock and pour over the beef in the slow cooker. Add the cashews and cook for 4 hours on the high setting or 8 hours on low.

4   About 10 minutes before the end of the cooking time, stir in the baby corn. If you are using the holding feature on the slow cooker, cook the baby corn in a separate pan and stir in just before serving.

5   Serve the beef over noodles, garnished with the spring onions, chilli and coconut.

osso buco with gremolata and polenta

Meaning literally 'bone with a hole', the osso buco is sliced knuckle of veal with marrow inside the bone – any good butcher will supply it. I order mine from an online butcher as it comes vacuum-packed and I can freeze it until required.

serves **6** • prep time **20 mins** • cooking time **4 hours on high/8 hours on low**

1 kg osso buco or knuckle of veal
3 tbsp plain flour
4 tbsp olive oil
30 g butter
3 carrots, chopped
3 celery sticks, chopped
2 onions, chopped
500 ml dry white wine
1 bay leaf

3 tbsp chopped thyme
1 x 400 g can chopped tomatoes
Grated zest of 2 lemons
1 garlic clove, finely chopped
2 tbsp chopped parsley
Salt and freshly ground black pepper
Quick cook polenta, to serve
3 tbsp extra virgin olive oil

1 Season the osso buco and toss in the flour.

2 Heat half the oil with half the butter in a large frying pan over a medium heat and cook the osso buco for 10 minutes, until browned. Transfer to the slow cooker.

3 Heat the remaining oil in the pan over a medium heat and cook the carrots, celery and onions for 5 minutes, until softened. Pour on the wine, let it bubble for a minute to deglaze the pan of the residue left from browning the veal and gather up all the flavour. Add the vegetables and sauce to the slow cooker, tucking half the vegetables under the veal. Add the bay leaf, thyme and tomatoes and season well, making sure all the flavours are spread around. Cook for 4 hours on the high setting or 8 hours on low.

4 To make the gremolata, mix together the lemon zest, garlic and parsley.

5 Make the polenta according to the packet instructions, then stir in the olive oil. Serve immediately with the osso buco, and hand the gremolata around separately.

veal stew with polenta

Veal shoulder becomes beautifully tender and moist in a slow cooker. In this dish the wine releases all its aromas into the braising liquid as the stew gently cooks, so make sure you use a good-quality white wine that has a significant but not overpowering flavour.

serves **6** • prep time **10 mins** • cooking time **4 hours on high/8 hours on low**

1 kg veal shoulder, diced
4 tbsp olive oil
1 tbsp flour
2 turnips, diced
2 onions, diced
2 celery stalks, diced
1 bay leaf
2 sprigs thyme leaves

200 ml hot chicken stock
200 ml white wine
250 g quick-cook polenta, to serve
2 tbsp extra virgin olive oil, to serve
4 tbsp finely chopped flat-leaf parsley
Sea salt and freshly ground
   black pepper

1 Season the meat. Heat half the oil in a large frying pan over a high heat and brown the veal. Transfer to the slow cooker and stir in the flour.

2 Heat the remaining oil in the frying pan over a high heat and cook the turnips, onions and celery for 5 minutes until softened. Transfer to the slow cooker.

3 Stir in the bay leaf, thyme, stock and white wine. Season well and cook for 4 hours on the high setting or 8 hours on low.

4 About 10 minutes before serving, cook the polenta according to the packet instructions and stir through some seasoning and the extra virgin olive oil.

5 Serve the veal stew spooned over the polenta, and garnished with the parsley.

venison braised with blueberry and juniper

In an effort to promote less intensive farming and encourage us to eat a wider variety of meats, butchers are selling much more venison. As it can be tough, it needs time to draw out its succulence, which is why slow cooking is ideal. Juniper berries are widely available from supermarkets and grocers.

serves **6** • prep time **15 mins** • cooking time **4 hours on high/8 hours on low**

4 tbsp **sunflower oil**
900 g **venison, diced**
2 tbsp **plain flour**
100 ml **port**
300 ml **red wine**
500 ml **beef or game stock**
6 **shallots**
1 **onion, diced**
2 **carrots, diced**
1 **celery stick, diced**

1 **bay leaf**
3 **thyme sprigs**
50 g **dried blueberries**
2 tsp **juniper berries**
Salt and freshly ground black pepper
6 **portobello or field mushrooms,**
    cleaned
3 tbsp **olive oil**
2 tbsp **chopped flat-leaf parsley**

1 Heat half the oil over a high heat in a large frying pan and cook the venison for about 5 minutes, until browned all over. Season and then stir in the flour. Add the port and let it bubble to deglaze the pan of any residue, then add the wine and the stock. Transfer the mixture to the slow cooker.

2 Heat the remaining oil over a medium heat in the pan and cook the shallots, onion, carrots and celery for about 10 minutes, until softened. Season and add the bay leaf and thyme. Transfer to the slow cooker.

3 Stir in the blueberries and juniper berries. Cook for 4 hours on the high setting or 8 hours on low.

4 To cook the mushrooms, preheat the grill or oven to 200°C/Gas 6. Set out the mushrooms on a baking tray, drizzle with the olive oil and season well. Grill or bake for 10 minutes and sprinkle with parsley. Serve hot with the braised venison.

mixed game stew with root vegetable mash

Look out for packs of mixed or individual game in the fresh meat section of supermarkets. These packs are available mainly in the autumn, but some game is to be found all year round. Good butchers will easily be able to supply an assortment of game to suit your personal taste and pocket. The usual mix would be venison, pigeon, quail and rabbit, but this varies according to season.

serves **6** • prep time **15 mins** • cooking time **4 hours on high/8 hours on low**

800 g mixed game, diced
160 g butter
1 tbsp plain flour
50 ml port
200 ml red wine
1 bay leaf
2 tbsp chopped thyme
2 garlic cloves, chopped
18 shallots, halved
700 g carrots, diced
2 celery sticks, chopped

200 ml game stock
Salt and freshly ground black pepper
1.5 kg potatoes, diced
500 g celeriac, diced
250 g button mushrooms, wiped
    clean and halved
3 tbsp crème fraîche
150 g pancetta, diced
2 tbsp chopped flat-leaf parsley,
    to garnish

1 Season the game. Heat 30 g of the butter over a medium heat in a large frying pan and cook the game for about 10 minutes, until sealed. Stir in the flour, then add the port and wine. Let it bubble for about 1 minute to deglaze any pan residue and take up the flavour, and then add the bay leaf and thyme. Transfer to the slow cooker.

2 Heat a further 30 g of the butter over a medium heat in the pan and cook the garlic, shallots, 200g of the carrots and celery for about 5 minutes, until softened. Add the stock and transfer to the slow cooker. Cook for 4 hours on the high setting or 8 hours on low.

3 To make the root vegetable mash, put the potatoes, remaining carrots and the celeriac in a pan of salted water and bring to the boil. Boil for about 20 minutes or until very tender. Drain the vegetables, and mash well, adding more seasoning. Stir in the remaining butter, and keep warm.

4 About 10 minutes before the end of the cooking time, add the mushrooms and crème fraîche to the game casserole. Then fry the pancetta in a dry pan over a medium heat, stirring constantly.

5 Serve the game stew with the root vegetable mash and garnish with chopped flat-leaf parsley and the fried pancetta.

slow-cooked rabbit with parsley and garlic

One of the joys of slow cooking is to transform tough cuts of meat into melt-in-the-mouth dishes through tender loving cooking. To discourage intensive farming, we should make an effort to vary the kinds of meats that we eat. Try cooking rabbit in the slow cooker, and be ready to put it on your shopping list more often. Rabbit needs a rich sauce, and in this recipe the lashings of olive oil bring the flavours of the naturally lean rabbit to life.

serves **4** • prep time **15 mins** • cooking time **4 hours on high/8 hours on low**

1 kg rabbit pieces, or 1 whole rabbit, jointed
4 tbsp olive oil
150 g pancetta, diced
4 garlic cloves, crushed
2 onions, chopped
2 carrots, diced

100 ml white wine
100 ml hot chicken stock
1 bay leaf
15 g flat-leaf parsley, chopped
Salt and freshly ground black pepper
500 g gnocchi, to serve

1   Season the rabbit. Heat half the oil in a large frying pan over a high heat and brown the rabbit and pancetta well. Transfer to the slow cooker.

2   Heat the remaining oil in the frying pan over a medium heat and soften the garlic, onions and carrots. Transfer to the slow cooker.

3   Deglaze the pan with the wine, and add to the slow cooker with the stock and bay leaf. Season well and cook for 4 hours on the high setting or 8 hours on low.

4   Just before serving, cook the gnocchi according to the packet instructions. Stir the parsley into the rabbit sauce and serve hot, spooned over the drained gnocchi.

venison and chestnuts in red wine

The celery that you use in this dish should be of the green kind that is grown outdoors with the leaves still on; the pale white kind does not have enough pungency. You might need to peel off some of the outside strings.

serves **6** • prep time **15 mins** • cooking time **4 hours on high/8 hours on low**

2 tbsp sunflower oil
40 g butter
12 shallots
2 carrots, diced
3 celery sticks, diced
1 onion, diced
750 g venison, diced
200 g streaky bacon, each rasher
   cut into three
2 tbsp plain flour

200 ml red wine
50 ml port
1 bay leaf
3 thyme sprigs
200 ml beef stock
200 g cooked and peeled chestnuts
200 g button mushrooms, wiped clean
Salt and freshly ground black pepper
Greens, to serve

1 Heat half the oil and butter over a medium heat in a large frying pan and cook the shallots, carrots, celery and onion for about 10 minutes, until softened. Season and spoon into the slow cooker.

2 Heat the remaining oil and butter in the pan over a high heat and cook the venison and bacon for 5 minutes, until browned all over. Season and stir the flour into the pan.

3 Stir in the wine and port, scraping up any residue from its base. Simmer for 5 minutes and pour into the slow cooker, adding the bay leaf and thyme.

4 Add the stock and cooked chestnuts to the slow cooker and cook for 4 hours on the high setting or 8 hours on low.

5 About 10 minutes before the end of the cooking time, add the mushrooms to the casserole and check the seasoning.

6 Serve the venison in red wine on warmed plates together with the greens.

WEEKEND
POT ROASTS

garlic and herb-stuffed chicken

This is a dish for all seasons – it is delicious served hot in the colder months with fresh crusty bread for mopping up the juices, but it also lends itself perfectly to the summer, served cold with a crisp green salad and seasonal new potatoes.

serves **6** • prep time **15 mins** • cooking time **4 hours on high/8 hours on low**

100 g butter
2 tbsp chopped flat-leaf parsley
2 tbsp chopped thyme
3 garlic cloves, crushed

2 kg chicken
100 ml white wine (optional)
Salt and freshly ground black pepper

1 Mash together the butter, herbs, garlic and seasoning. Take the skin of the chicken breast at the thickest part and pull it away from the meat. Using your fingertips, push the garlic and herb butter in between the skin and breast, as far along as you can, so that the whole chicken gets basted. Be careful towards the centre of the breast, as the skin is thin here and can tear easily.

2 Set the chicken in the slow cooker and pour the wine into the bottom. Cover and cook for 4 hours on the high setting or 8 hours on low.

3 Remove the chicken from the cooker. Serve hot with the buttery juices spooned over or cold, simply sliced, depending on your preference!

Note: Suitable for 6 litre model; for the 3 litre size, use a 1.2 kg chicken

butter-basted whole chicken
with lemon and thyme

When chicken is cooked this way, it is succulent and full of flavour remaining moist even when cooked. Try serving it at room temperature in the warmer months with a crunchy selection of summer vegetables.

serves **8** • prep time **10 mins** • cooking time **4 hours on high/8 hours on low**

50 g butter
Juice and zest of 1 lemon
2 tbsp thyme leaves
1 x 2 kg chicken
150 ml chicken stock
3 tbsp cornflour

2 tbsp chopped parsley (optional)
Salt and freshly ground black pepper
Sugar snap peas, to serve
Baby carrots, to serve
Mangetout, to serve

1 Mash together the butter, lemon juice and zest, thyme and salt and pepper. Using your fingerts, push the butter in between the skin and breast of the chicken or rub it all over the chicken breast.

2 Place the chicken in the slow cooker and pour the stock into the bottom. Cover and cook for 4 hours on the high setting or 8 hours on low.

3 Remove chicken from the cooker and set aside to keep warm while you make the sauce.

4 To make the sauce, spoon off the excess fat from the cooking liquid and place the remaining juices in a pan over a medium heat. Mix the cornflour in a cup with a little water and then stir into the gravy together with the parsley, if using, and bring to a simmer to thicken. Simmer for 3–4 minutes, to cook the cornflour and allow the flavours to mellow, before serving with the chicken and vegetables.

rice-stuffed shoulder of lamb

Lamb is the ideal meat for a slow-cooked pot roast, as it becomes succulent and releases all its flavour. You will get the best flavour if you brown the lamb before adding it to the slow cooker, but if time does not allow, it will still turn golden during cooking. If you can't get shoulder, a boned leg of lamb also works well in this recipe.

serves **6** • prep time **15 mins** • cooking time **4 hours on high/8 hours on low**

1 kg shoulder of lamb, boned
2 tbsp olive oil
2 garlic cloves, sliced
1 lemon, roughly chopped
100 g easy-cook or
   parboiled white rice, cooked

10 sun-dried tomatoes, halved
100 ml white wine
500 g waxy potatoes, cut into large dice
Salt and freshly ground black pepper
You will need 2 metal skewers

1 Season the lamb all over. Heat the oil in a large frying pan over a high heat, and brown the lamb on the outside. (This can be tricky, as the lamb will not be a neat shape.)

2 Remove from the heat and leave the lamb in the pan. In the larger muscles at either end of the joint, make a deep incision to divide the piece into two. Insert some of the garlic and lemon in these deep incisions, and tuck the rest into the remaining meat. Spoon over half of the rice, pushing it into the incisions, and add the sun-dried tomatoes. Now fold the joint in two, with the opening uppermost, and secure with the metal skewers. Spoon over the remaining rice, pushing it into the opening. Push as much of the filling that has fallen out back into the opening. Transfer the lamb to the slow cooker.

3 Return the frying pan to the heat and add the wine to the pan juices. Heat until just sizzling then pour the pan contents over the lamb. Add the potatoes to the slow cooker, season well, and cook for 4 hours on the high setting or 8 hours on low.

4 Serve the lamb and the rice together, with the diced potatoes.

herby garlic-roasted lamb

Long slow cooking gently tenderises this premium lamb joint, and it tastes particularly good with garlic, as the flavours blend together and become milder. A real taste of the Mediterranean for a lazy weekend lunch in the sun.

serves **6** • prep time **15 mins** • cooking time **4 hours on high/8 hours on low**

1 kg leg of lamb
2 tbsp olive oil
1 garlic head
15 g flat-leaf parsley
15 g thyme

½ lemon, chopped
100 ml white wine
1 kg potatoes, peeled and halved
Salt and freshly ground black pepper

1 Season the lamb all over. Heat the oil in a large frying pan over a high heat and brown the lamb on the outside. (This can be tricky, as the lamb will not be a neat shape.)

2 Slice the garlic in half horizontally and place the pieces in the slow cooker. Chop together the herbs with some seasoning and add to the slow cooker. Add the lemon and pour over the wine.

3 Transfer the lamb to the slow cooker and cook for 4 hours on the high setting or 8 hours on low.

4 When cooked, remove the lamb using a carving fork and strain the juices left behind in the slow cooker through a sieve into a jug. Spoon off any excess fat in the juices and check the seasoning.

5 Serve the lamb and juices together, with simple potatoes.

traditional pot-roasted beef
with fresh herb dumplings

In this traditional dish, long slow cooking renders an otherwise tough cut of beef succulent and creates a rich, silky sauce with layers of flavour.

serves **6** • prep time **15 mins** • cooking time **4 hours on high/8 hours on low**

1.4 kg stewing steak, diced
50 g butter or sunflower spread
2 tbsp plain flour
500 ml beef stock
1 bay leaf
1 large thyme sprig
1 rosemary sprig
4 onions, diced

3 carrots, diced
2 celery sticks, diced
100 g vegetable suet
100 g self-raising flour
3 tbsp chopped mixed herbs
Salt and freshly ground black pepper
Green vegetables, to serve

1 Season the beef. Heat half the butter over a high heat in a large frying pan and cook the beef for about 5 minutes, in batches if necessary, until browned all over. Stir in the plain flour, then spoon the mixture into the slow cooker.

2 Pour a little of the stock into the pan and use a wooden spoon to scrape off any residue. Transfer to the slow cooker together with the bay leaf, thyme and rosemary.

3 Heat the remaining butter over a medium heat in the pan and cook the onions, carrots and celery for about 10 minutes, until softened. Transfer to the slow cooker and add the remaining stock. Cook for 4 hours on the high setting or 8 hours on low.

4 Start making the dumplings about 20 minutes before the end of the cooking time. Combine the suet, self-raising flour and mixed herbs in a bowl and add seasoning. Stir in 200 ml water until a dough forms, then drop teaspoons of the dough on top of the casserole. Cover and cook for 15 minutes.

5 Serve hot with the green vegetables of your choice.

mustard-crusted roast beef with parsnips

This is a classic Sunday lunch in one pot, using the traditional English flavours that complement beef: strong English mustard and hearty sweet parsnips. If you're going all out for the full 'roast' lunch, serve this with creamy mashed potatoes and steamed green cabbage.

serves **6** • prep time **30 minutes** • cooking time **4 hours on high/8 hours on low**

3 tbsp English mustard powder
3 tbsp soft light brown sugar
1.3 kg beef topside or brisket joint
4 tbsp olive oil
2 onions, peeled and cut into wedges
100 ml hot beef stock

2 tbsp chopped thyme leaves
4 parsnips, peeled and halved
   lengthways
2 tbsp cornflour, made into a paste with
   a little cold water
Salt and freshly ground black pepper

1 Mix together the mustard powder and sugar and season well. Press the paste into the fat on the beef joint.

2 Heat half the oil in a large frying pan over a high heat and brown the onions for 5 minutes. Transfer to the slow cooker.

3 Heat the remaining oil in the frying pan over a high heat and cook the beef until well browned. Transfer to the slow cooker. Pour a little of the stock into the frying pan and use a wooden spoon to scrape off any residue, then add to the slow cooker.

4 Add the parsnips to the slow cooker, arranging them around the edge, then cook for 4 hours on the high setting or 8 hours on low.

5 Lift out the beef and parsnips using a carving fork and a slotted spoon onto a serving dish and cover while you make the gravy. Sieve the juices in the slow cooker into a pan. Bring the liquid to a simmer, stir in the cornflour paste and simmer for 2 minutes to thicken slightly. Check the seasoning.

6 Serve the beef and gravy with vegetables of your choice.

pot-roasted beef

with rosemary, thyme and anchovies

Slowly pot-roasting a beef joint allows the meat juices to soak into the potatoes, infusing them with flavour and leaving the beef beautifully succulent and tender. This is a truly wonderful one-pot winter warmer.

serves **6** • prep time **30 minutes** • cooking time **4 hours on high/8 hours on low**

4 tbsp olive oil
1.3 kg beef topside or brisket joint
200 ml hot beef stock
100 ml red wine
2 onions, peeled and roughly chopped
25 g anchovies in olive oil

25 g rosemary leaves
15 g thyme leaves
750 g waxy potatoes, peeled and thickly sliced
Freshly ground black pepper

1 Heat half the oil in a large frying pan over a high heat. Season the beef with a little pepper and cook it for about 10 minutes until well browned on all sides. Set aside to cool. Pour a little of the stock into the frying pan and use a wooden spoon to scrape off any residue. Transfer the liquid to the slow cooker along with the wine.

2 Heat the remaining oil in the frying pan and brown the onions. Transfer to the slow cooker.

3 Chop together the anchovies, rosemary and thyme and stuff this mixture into the beef. Place the beef in the slow cooker.

4 Put the potatoes around the beef joint and cook for 4 hours on the high setting or 8 hours on low.

piquant teriyaki pot-roasted beef

This simple beef dish makes a light and slightly spicy alternative to a roast. Serve with steamed green leaves, such as pak choi, to complement the Eastern flavours.

serves **6** • prep time **15 mins** • cooking time **4 hours on high/8 hours on low**

6 spring onions
3 carrots, peeled
1 red pepper, seeded
1.4 kg beef brisket joint
2 tbsp sunflower oil

150 ml teriyaki marinade
Egg noodles, to serve
3 tbsp coriander leaves
3 tbsp finely chopped chives
Salt and freshly ground black pepper

1 Cut the spring onions in half, then cut the carrots in half lengthways, and then half again. Cut the pepper into similar-sized strips. Put all the vegetables into the slow cooker.

2 Season the beef. Heat the oil in a large frying pan over a high heat and brown the beef. Transfer it to the slow cooker, pour over the teriyaki marinade and cook for 4 hours on the high setting or 8 hours on low. Keep basting as often as possible.

3 About 10 minutes before the end of cooking, cook the noodles according to the packet instructions.

4 Slice the beef and serve witht he onions, carrots and pepper. Garnish the beef teriyaki with the coriander and chives, and serve piping hot with the sauce spooned over the noodles.

sesame-roasted pork shoulder

Sweet roasted sesame seeds are fantastic with pork, adding a depth of flavour to the meat and the sauce. Serve it with plain long grain rice and steamed vegetables, such as broccoli, to offset the richness of the dish.

serves **6** • prep time **20 mins** • cooking time **4 hours on high/8 hours on low**

1 tbsp sunflower oil
2 carrots, diced
1 red onion, diced
1.3 kg pork shoulder joint, skin removed
3 garlic cloves, peeled

100 ml hot chicken stock
50 g clear honey
100 g sesame seeds
2 tsp English mustard powder
Salt and freshly ground black pepper

1 Heat the oil in a large frying pan over a high heat and cook the carrots and onion for 3 minutes or so until just softened. Spoon into the slow cooker.

2 Season the pork joint and brown it all over in the same pan, without oil. Transfer to the slow cooker with the garlic, stock, honey and seasoning.

3 In a dry pan over a medium heat, roast the sesame seeds until aromatic. Scatter them over the pork joint and cook for 4 hours on the high setting or 8 hours on low.

4 To serve, remove the pork and strain the sauce in the slow cooker into a pan. Boil the sauce for 5 minutes to reduce.

5 Slice the pork, and serve with the sauce and rice or vegetables.

slow-roasted pork belly with star anise

This is a delicate, Chinese-spiced dish that will melt in the mouth after lengthy cooking. However, if you prefer more texture, cook this ahead of time then remove the pork belly slices and roast them for 20 minutes at 220°C/gas 7 just before serving so that they crisp up; then serve them separately to the broth.

serves **6** • prep time **15 mins** • cooking time **4 hours on high/8 hours on low**

2 tbsp sesame oil
1.5 kg boneless belly of pork, rind removed
6 spring onions, left whole
3 carrots, roughly chopped
2 garlic cloves, chopped

4 star anise
100 ml hot chicken stock
100 ml rice wine
3 heads pak choi, quartered
Rice noodles, cooked to serve

1 Heat the oil in a large frying pan over a high heat. Add the pork and cook for 5 minutes, turning often, until browned. Transfer to the slow cooker.

2 Add the remaining ingredients to the slow cooker and cook for 4 hours on the high setting or 8 hours on low.

3 About 5 minutes before the end of cooking time, add the pak choi and stir through.

4 Serve the broth and the pak choi in bowls with the rice noodles and with the pork belly on a separate serving dish.

PUDDINGS AND DESSERTS

tiramisu sponge desserts

This is a great make-ahead dessert – and in fact it tastes better if you allow some time for setting it aside for the flavours to develop. For those who do not like coffee, simply leave it out of the topping.

serves **6** • prep time **10 mins** • cooking time **4 hours on high/8 hours on low**

100 g caster sugar
100 g butter
2 eggs, beaten
50 g grated chocolate
25 g cocoa powder, sieved,
   plus extra to decorate

75 g self-raising flour
250 g mascarpone cheese
2 tbsp icing sugar, sifted
3 tbsp liquid coffee, i.e. Camp
1 tsp vanilla extract
You will need 6 x 150 ml ramekins

1 Beat the sugar and butter together until creamy and smooth, then beat in the eggs slowly, until smooth. Add the chocolate and stir in the cocoa powder. Lastly, stir in the flour.

2 Divide the mixture between the ramekins. Put 3–4 layers of greaseproof paper in the base of the slow cooker and put the ramekins on top, stacking if necessary. Pour in hot water to a depth of about 2 cm and cook for 4 hours on the high setting or 8 hours on low. Allow to cool.

3 To serve, beat together the mascarpone, icing sugar, liquid coffee and vanilla extract until smooth. Spoon a little of this mixture over the top of each chocolate base, sieve over some cocoa powder and serve.

butterscotch rice pudding

Butterscotch is a flavour that takes me straight back to childhood –
in my case to those 'just-add-milk' mousse desserts that my mum would
whip up out of a packet. Delicious as they were to me then, with my
slightly more sophisticated adult tastes, this home-made butterscotch
beats those hands down for flavour.

serves **6** • prep time **20 mins** • cooking time **4 hours on high/8 hours on low**

120 g soft light brown sugar
50 g golden syrup
50 g butter

130 g pudding rice
1.2 litres full-fat milk

1 Mix together the sugar and golden syrup in a pan over a medium heat
and cook for about 5 minutes until the sugar is dissolved. Add the butter and
stir until smooth.

2 Pour the mixture into the slow cooker with the milk and, lastly, stir in the rice.

3 Cook for 4 hours on the high setting or 8 hours on low.

almond and passion fruit bake

Do not serve this dessert to friends and expect to have leftovers. It is a real treat – rich, a little decadent, but divine. All you need with it is some single cream and perhaps a little lie down on the sofa afterwards!

serves **6** • prep time **15 mins** • cooking time **4 hours on high/8 hours on low**

150 g butter
100 g light brown soft sugar
? tsp almond extract
3 eggs, beaten
150 g self-raising flour
100 g ground almonds

100 ml passion fruit juice
50 g caster sugar
2 fresh passion fruit, to serve
You will need 6 x 150 ml ramekins,
   or a 1 litre pudding basin

1   Beat the butter together with the sugar until pale and creamy. Add the almond extract.

2   Beat in the eggs, one at a time, then fold in the flour and stir in the ground almonds. Divide the mixture between the ramekins or place in the pudding basin.

3   Cover the ramekins or pudding basin with foil. If you are using a single pudding bowl you will need a strap made from a length of foil, folded over a few times for strength, that runs underneath the bowl to make it easier to lift out of the slow cooker at the end. Place the ramekin or bowl into the slow cooker, stacking if necessary, and pour in boiling water to a depth of 1–2 cm. Cook for 4 hours on the high setting or 8 hours on low.

4   Meanwhile, in a pan over a medium heat, stir together the pasion fruit juice and sugar until the sugar is dissolved. When the pudding is cooked, remove from the slow cooker, skewer the surface all over and spoon over the syrup, allowing it to drain down into the pudding. Serve warm with a few pieces of passion fruit spooned over each dessert.

toffee and pecan pudding

This pairing of flavours is a perennial favourite. If you want to vary the basic recipe you could try adding a pinch of ground ginger to the mix.

serves **8** • prep time **20 mins** • cooking time **4 hours on high/8 hours on low**

200 g pitted dates
1 tsp bicarbonate of soda
1 tbsp golden syrup
120 g light muscovado sugar
300 g softened butter, plus extra
   for greasing

100 g pecans, roughly chopped
175 g soft dark brown sugar
2 eggs
175 g self-raising flour
Single cream, to serve

1 Put the dates in a saucepan, cover with water and bring to the boil. Add the bicarbonate of soda, which breaks down the skin of the dates and tenderises them, making them easier to digest, and simmer for 5 minutes. Drain well and set aside.

2 To make the sticky toffee sauce, place the syrup, light muscovado sugar and 120 g of the butter in a clean pan and simmer over a gentle heat, together for about 10 minutes, until dissolved. Meanwhile, grease six 150 ml ramekins or a 1 litre pudding bowl that fits your slow cooker. Divide the pecans among the ramekins or place in the pudding bowl. Spoon a little sauce into the prepared bowl(s).

3 For the sponge, beat together the remaining butter, the dark brown sugar, eggs and flour until creamy. Stir the dates into the mixture.

4 Pour the sponge mix into the ramekins or bowl and cover with foil. If using a pudding bowl, you will also need a 'strap' made from a length of foil, folded over a few times for strength, that goes under the bowl to make it easier to lift out of the slow cooker.

5 Put the dishes into the slow cooker, stacking them if necessary. Pour in boiling water to a depth of 1–2 cm, but not more than halfway up the sides of the ramekins. Cook for 4 hours on the high setting or 8 hours on low. Serve warm with single cream.

individual caramelised pear and mascarpone cheesecakes

The cleverest thing about this scrumptious dessert is that the base can be used with any other topping, not just the caramelised pear that I have recommended here; try fresh raspberries with granola, or chopped peaches doused in Italian vin santo wine.

serves **6** • prep time **10 mins** • cooking time **4 hours on high/8 hours on low**

120 g digestive biscuits	**2 large eggs, beaten**
50 g butter, melted	**30 g butter, to serve**
300 g mascarpone cheese	**3 small firm pears, to serve**
100 g caster sugar	**30 g demerara sugar, to serve**
1 tsp vanilla extract	**You will need 6 x 150 ml ramekins**

1 First, crush the biscuits. The easiest way to do this is to place the biscuits in a strong food bag and crush them with a rolling pin.

2 Mix the crumbs with the melted butter and press the mixture into the ramekins, smoothing the surface with a spoon.

3 Whisk together the mascarpone, sugar, vanilla and eggs in a large bowl until the mixture is smooth, then divide the mix between the ramekins. Cover each dish with foil. Put 3–4 layers of greaseproof paper in the base of the slow cooker and put the covered ramekins on top, stacking if necessary. Pour in hot water to a depth of about 2 cm, cover, and cook for 4 hours on the high setting or 8 hours on low. Allow to cool.

4 To serve, melt the butter in a large frying pan over a medium heat. Peel, core and either slice or chop the pears and add them to the pan. Sprinkle them with the sugar and cook for 5 minutes, or until the sugar is dissolved. Spoon the pears onto the cheesecakes and serve.

pistachio and lemon rice pudding

This is one of those recipes that I can never make enough of. If it doesn't all get eaten immediately, I can guarantee that someone will be enjoying it the next day, reheated with chocolate spread stirred though it! Do experiment with your own flavourings: you could try adding a spoonful of drinking chocolate or ground cinnamon to the milk, or stirring through some chopped nuts just before serving.

serves **6** • prep time **20 mins** • cooking time **4 hours on high/8 hours on low**

130 g pudding rice	Rind from 1 lemon, in one piece
15 g sugar	1.2 litres full-fat milk
120 g flaked almonds, toasted	

1 Put the rice in the slow cooker and stir in the sugar, almonds and lemon rind.

2 Gently heat the milk in a saucepan until hot but not boiling and add to the slow cooker.

3 Cook for 4 hours on the high setting or 8 hours on low.

rhubarb and orange pudding

You will probably be surprised by the lightness of the sponge in this fragrant pudding. It is particularly delicious served with a big dollop of vanilla ice cream or lashings of creamy custard.

serves **6** • prep time **15 mins** • cooking time **4 hours on high/8 hours on low**

225 g rhubarb, chopped into 2 cm
   pieces
3 tbsp demerara sugar
Grated zest of 2 oranges
150 g butter, plus extra for greasing

80 g dark brown soft sugar
80 g light brown soft sugar
3 eggs
120 g self-raising flour
Vanilla ice cream or custard, to serve

1 Place the rhubarb, demerara sugar and half the grated orange zest in a bowl and stir well.

2 Grease six 150 ml ramekins or a 1 litre pudding bowl that fits your slow cooker..

3 In a clean bowl and using an electric hand whisk, beat together the butter and brown sugars until pale and creamy. Beat in the eggs, one at a time, then fold in the flour and stir in the remaining zest.

4 Cover the ramekins or pudding bowl with foil. If using a pudding bowl, you will also need a 'strap' made from a length of foil, folded over a few times for strength, that goes under the bowl to make it easier to lift out of the slow cooker. Put into the slow cooker, stacking them if necessary, and pour in boiling water to a depth of 1–2 cm, but not more than halfway up the sides of the ramekins. Cook for 4 hours on the high setting or 8 hours on low.

5 Serve the puddings warm with vanilla ice cream or custard.

baked cherry cheesecake

Baked cheesecake is one of my favourite indulgences, and slow cooking is perfect for it as it prevents drying out. This cheesecake has an irresistibly moist filling set over a buttery biscuit base and is delicious served warm or cold. (I have made the cheesecake filling lower in fat in order to pack the base with lovely butter.)

serves **8** • prep time **10 mins** • cooking time **4 hours on high/8 hours on low**

150 g digestive biscuits
50 g ratafia biscuits
100 g butter
300 g half-fat soft cheese
200 g quark cheese or strained cottage
  cheese

150 g caster sugar
1 tsp vanilla extract
3 large eggs, beaten
1 x 400 g can cherries in syrup, drained
  and dried on kitchen paper

1   Crush the digestive and ratafia biscuits by placing them in a strong food bag and flattening with a rolling pin.

2   Put the butter in a saucepan over a low heat and gently melt. Tip in the crushed biscuits and mix together. Press the biscuits into eight 150 ml ramekin dishes smoothing the surface with the back of a spoon.

3   In a large bowl, whisk together the cheeses, sugar, vanilla and eggs until the mixture is smooth. Spoon on to the biscuit bases, stopping about 1 cm below the rim.

4   Divide the drained cherries between the ramekins and cover with foil.

5   Put the ramekins on a rack in the bottom of the slow cooker. If no rack is available, line the cooker with four layers of baking parchment or greaseproof paper and sit the dishes on that. Pour in hot water to a depth of about 2 cm, but not more than halfway up the sides of the ramekins. Cook for 4 hours on the high setting or 6 hours on low.

chocolate custard pots

This will delight all chocoholics – my daughter thought it was chocolate heaven. If you prefer an even more intense flavour, simply increase the amount of chocolate by 50 g.

serves **6** • prep time **5 mins** • cooking time **4 hours on high/8 hours on low**

Butter, for greasing
3 eggs
2 egg yolks
50 g caster sugar
400 ml milk

100 ml double cream
200 g plain chocolate, grated
300 g strawberries or raspberries,
   to decorate
150 ml whipping cream, to serve

1 Grease six 150 ml ramekins or a 1 litre pudding bowl that fits into your slow cooker.

2 Place the eggs, egg yolks and sugar in a bowl and beat together with an electric mixer until pale.

3 In a saucepan, gently heat the milk and cream together until very hot, but not boiling.

4 Stir the chocolate into the milk, then pour in the beaten eggs, whisking continuously. Pour the mixture into the ramekins or pudding bowl and cover with foil. Put a rack in the bottom of the slow cooker, or line it with four layers of baking parchment or greaseproof paper. Sit the bowl or ramekins on this, stacking if necessary. Pour in boiling water to a depth of 2 cm, but not more than halfway up the sides of the ramekins. Cook for 4 hours on the high setting or 8 hours on low.

5 To serve warm, put each ramekin on a plate decorated with a few berries, and hand around the cream in a jug. To serve cold, whip the cream and pipe or spoon on top of the ramekins. Put each one on a plate, together with a few berries.
If serving in a large bowl, hand around the berries and cream separately.

poached vanilla pears with maple biscuits

Hard pears work best for this old favourite as they hold their shape better than soft ones. They are particularly delicious drizzled with a chocolate sauce, and the biscuits are an easy addition if you have the time and inclination, or if the oven is on.

serves **6** • prep time **15 mins** • cooking time **4 hours on low**

6 hard pears, such as Packham or Comice
150 g granulated sugar
2 vanilla pods, split
5 tbsp clear honey
375 ml sweet wine

25 g butter
2 tbsp maple syrup
1 tbsp caster sugar
50 g plain flour
1 egg white

1 Stand the pears in the slow cooker.

2 In a saucepan over a gentle heat, dissolve the sugar in 100 ml of water, then pour over the pears. Add the vanilla pods, honey and wine. Cook for 4 hours on the low setting, although they can be held for a further 2 hours if necessary.

3 Transfer the pears to a bowl and the syrup to a saucepan. Let the sauce simmer to reduce to a syrupy consistency. (It can also be used as it is.)

4 To make the biscuits, preheat the oven to 200°C/Gas 6 and line a baking sheet with non-stick baking parchment or grease and flour. Put the butter, maple syrup and caster sugar in a bowl and beat together with an electric whisk. Stir in the flour. In a separate bowl, beat the egg white until softly stiff, and fold into the butter mixture.

5 Drop teaspoonfuls of the biscuit mixture on to the prepared baking sheet spaced well apart (you should make about 12 biscuits) and bake for about 8 minutes, until golden. Remove and cool on a rack.

6 Serve the pears with a little syrup drizzled over and with 2 biscuits on the side.

sticky toffee pudding

If you want to vary the basic recipe for this perennial favourite, you could try adding chopped pecans or a pinch of ground ginger to the mix.

serves **8** • prep time **20 mins** • cooking time **4 hours on high/8 hours on low**

200 g pitted dates, chopped
1 tsp bicarbonate of soda
1 tbsp golden syrup
120 g light muscovado sugar
300 g softened butter, plus extra
    for greasing

175 g soft dark brown sugar
2 eggs
175 g self-raising flour
Single cream, to serve

1 Put the dates in a saucepan, cover with water and bring to the boil. Add the bicarbonate of soda, which breaks down the skin of the dates and tenderises them, making them easier to digest, and simmer for 5 minutes. Drain well and set aside.

2 To make the sticky toffee sauce, place the syrup, light muscovado sugar and 120 g of the butter in a clean pan and simmer over a gentle heat, together for about 10 minutes, until dissolved. Meanwhile, grease six 150 ml ramekins or a 1 litre pudding bowl that fits your slow cooker. Spoon a little sauce into the prepared bowl(s).

3 For the sponge, beat together the remaining butter, the dark brown sugar, eggs and flour until creamy. Stir the dates into the mixture.

4 Pour the sponge mix into the ramekins or bowl and cover with foil. If using a pudding bowl, you will also need a 'strap' made from a length of foil, folded over a few times for strength, that goes under the bowl to make it easier to lift out of the slow cooker.

5 Put the dishes into the slow cooker, stacking them if necessary. Pour in boiling water to a depth of 1–2 cm, but not more than halfway up the sides of the ramekins. Cook for 4 hours on the high setting or 8 hours on low.

6 Serve warm with single cream.

PRESERVES

orange marmalade

Seville oranges are in season for only two weeks in January. Sadly, this never seems to coincide with me finding the time to make marmalade so the tinned Seville oranges are a brilliant substitute. Not only do they mean that this marmalade can be made at any time of the year, but you are also spared the task of preparing them. The tinned oranges are widely available at most supermarkets.

makes **6 jars** • prep time **10 mins** • cooking time **8 hours on low**

1 x 850 g can thin-cut Seville oranges
70 ml lemon juice

1.8 kg preserving sugar

1 Sterilise six clean jam jars with well-fitting lids by rinsing them out in very hot or boiling water. Drain on a clean tea towel until dry. Alternatively, put them in a dishwasher on the hot cycle.

2 Put all the ingredients into the slow cooker and pour over 400 ml of water. Cook for 8 hours on a low setting (don't be tempted to cook for 4 hours on a high setting because the marmalade will catch around the edges and still not be set).

3 When finished cooking, allow the marmalade to cool slightly before putting into jars to make it easier and safer to handle. Cover loosely with the lids and, when quite cool, tighten them. The marmalade will keep for up to three months if stored in a cool, dark place – the back of a cupboard is fine.

Variations
For whisky marmalade, add 2 teaspoons of whisky or a whisky liqueur per kg.
For ginger marmalade, add 2 teaspoons of chopped stem ginger per kg.

lemon curd

This lemon curd is wonderful on toast, but you could also use it to fill a pastry case for an indulgent lemon tart, or mini tart cases for fancy petit fours. If you want to experiment with the recipe, replace the lemon juice with lime or orange juice. Please note that it's important to measure out the correct weight of eggs for this recipe.

makes **about 5 jars** • prep time **15 mins** • cooking time **4 hours on low**

240 g butter
650 g caster sugar

330 ml lemon juice
 (from about 8 lemons)
300 ml fresh eggs (from about 5 eggs)

1 Sterilise five clean jam jars (see page 123).

2 In a saucepan, melt the butter over a gentle heat and stir in the sugar. Heat until the sugar is nearly dissolved, and then stir in the lemon juice. Do not boil, but stir until the sugar has melted. Remove from the heat and allow to cool for 5 minutes so that the eggs will not cook when added in the next step. To speed up the cooling process, sit the pan in a bowl of iced water.

3 Beat the eggs into the cooled butter mixture with a wooden spoon. When smooth, pour immediately into the prepared jars and screw on the lids.

4 Put the jars on a rack in the slow cooker. If no rack is available, sit the jars on four layers of baking parchment or greaseproof paper. Pour in boiling water to come halfway up the sides of the jars.

5 Cook the curd for 4 hours on a low setting and then set aside to cool. The finished lemon curd will keep in the refrigerator for up to three weeks.

spiced tomato chutney

Mi-cuit tomatoes are a great store cupboard ingredient. They are semi-dried and widely available in cans or boxes. The tomato flavour they deliver is better than sun-dried tomatoes and they are a great addition to anything tomatoey. Use sun-dried tomatoes if not available.

makes **6 jars** • prep time **25 mins** • cooking time **4 hours on high/8 hours on low**

1 kg tomatoes, cored and roughly
   chopped
1 tbsp salt
450 g onions
1 red chilli, deseeded and roughly
   chopped
5 garlic cloves
1 red pepper, deseeded and roughly
   chopped

100 g mi-cuit tomatoes
2 cooking apples
1 cinnamon stick
2 tsp mustard seeds
½ tsp freshly ground black pepper
½ tsp ground allspice
250 ml red wine vinegar
250 g soft dark brown sugar
150 g demerara sugar

1 Sterilise six clean jam jars (see page 123).

2 In a bowl, mix together the tomatoes and salt. Set a sieve over another bowl and spoon in the tomatoes. Leave to drain for 15 minutes, without pushing through.

3 Meanwhile, finely chop the onions, chilli, garlic and red pepper (this can be done in a food processor). Add to the slow cooker.

4 Process together the drained tomatoes, mi-cuit tomatoes and apples and add to the slow cooker.

5 In a saucepan over a gentle heat, warm the cinnamon, mustard seeds, black pepper and allspice for about 2 minutes, until they smell aromatic. Stir into the slow cooker. Cook for 4 hours on the high setting or 8 hours on low.

6 When finished cooking, allow the chutney to cool slightly before putting into jars. Cover loosely with the lids and, when quite cool, tighten them. The chutney will keep for up to three months if stored in a cool, dark place – the back of a cupboard is fine.

dried fruit compote

Fill your house with the comforting smell of spices in winter and remind everyone that Christmas is close. This compote is wonderfully versatile: it can be spooned over porridge at breakfast or flavoured with kirsch (cherry liqueur) and enjoyed with ice cream after dinner. You will need to buy the unsulphured dried fruit available in health food shops rather than the soft, ready-to-eat kind as the latter break down too much and retain no texture. Below is my preferred combination of fruit, but you might want to use a different mixture, such as cranberries and apple, or figs and apple. Steer clear of dried dates and strawberries, however, as these do not compote well.

makes **about 2 kg** • prep time **5 mins** • cooking time **4 hours on high/8 hours on low**

125 g dried sour cherries
250 g dried pear halves
125 g dried figs
250 g dried apricots
3 star anise

1 cinnamon stick
1 bay leaf
Pared rind of 2 oranges
600 ml cranberry juice
100 g clear honey

1 Put all the fruit together with the star anise, cinnamon, bay leaf and orange rind in the slow cooker and mix together.

2 In a saucepan, heat the cranberry juice and honey with 500 ml of water until nearly hot, and pour over the fruit. Cook for 4 hours on the high setting or 8 hours on low.

3 Serve the compote hot or cold. It will keep for up to five days if chilled, or can be frozen in small quantities.

index

aduki beans 121
almonds 67, 85, 144, 223,
    226
apple 141
    with duck 166
    with pork 88, 176
    in preserves 236, 237
aubergine:
    with chicken 152
    chilli 126
    curry 61

beans 53, 80, 121
    baked 178
    with beef 195
    in casseroles/stews 95,
        108, 120, 138, 144,
        192
    cassoulet 110
    with chicken 154, 162
    in chilli 113, 126, 143
    green 49, 59, 68, 78, 126,
        133, 170
    with meatballs 53
    in sauce 53, 102
    in soup 13, 32, 39
    see also by name
beef:
    with cashews 196
    in chianti 195
    Chinese 102
    goulash 39

mustard-crusted 212
    pot-roasted 210, 213
    Vietnamese 101
belly pork 92, 218
black beans 102, 113, 143,
    154
bolognese 98, 146
borlotti beans 192, 195
butter beans 31, 110, 120,
    144, 178
butternut squash 14, 130

cannellini beans 53, 108,
    138
cashews 122–4, 145, 196
casserole:
    bean 95, 110, 120
    beef 97
    chicken 70, 165
    game 104
    meatball 186
    pork 88, 89
    rabbit 106, 200–1
    sausage 95
    vegetable 136–7
cauliflower 34, 144
cheesecake 225, 228
chicken 38, 49, 50, 65, 68
    bake 162
    casserole 70, 165
    creamy 149
    curry 164

garlic-and-herb 206
    jalapeño 154
    jerk 165
    korma 75
    Mexican 162
    pasta 64
    with peppers 66
    piripiri 161
    soup 25, 36
    Spanish 158
    sweet and sour 163
    tagine 152
    tandoori 153
    tikka masala 150
    turkey alternative to 54
chickpea:
    curry 142
    lamb with 72
    soup 20, 34
chilli 113, 126, 143
chipotle 143
chocolate 220, 226, 230,
    231
chorizo 192
chowder 16
chutney 236
colcannon 190
compote 137
crayfish 44
curry:
    aubergine 61
    chicken 67, 150, 164